P9-DEP-706

WITHDRAWN

OPPOSING
VIEWPOINTS®
SERIES

# Gun Violence

# Other Books of Related Interest:

**Opposing Viewpoints Series**

Juvenile Crime

Organized Crime

**At Issue Series**

Guns and Crime

Self-Defense Laws

Violent Video Games

**Current Controversies Series**

Gangs

Violence in the Media

"Congress shall make
no law . . . abridging
the freedom of speech,
or of the press."

*First Amendment to the US Constitution*

The basic foundation of our democracy is the First Amendment guarantee of freedom of expression. The Opposing Viewpoints series is dedicated to the concept of this basic freedom and the idea that it is more important to practice it than to enshrine it.

# OPPOSING VIEWPOINTS® SERIES

# Gun Violence

*Noël Merino, Book Editor*

**GREENHAVEN PRESS**
*A part of Gale, Cengage Learning*

Farmington Hills, Mich • San Francisco • New York • Waterville, Maine
Meriden, Conn • Mason, Ohio • Chicago

364.15
GUN

GALE
CENGAGE Learning

Patricia Coryell, *Vice President & Publisher, New Products & GVRL*
Douglas Dentino, *Manager, New Products*
Judy Galens, *Acquisitions Editor*

© 2015 Greenhaven Press, a part of Gale, Cengage Learning.

WCN: 01-100-101

Gale and Greenhaven Press are registered trademarks used herein under license.

*For more information, contact:*
Greenhaven Press
27500 Drake Rd.
Farmington Hills, MI 48331-3535
Or you can visit our Internet site at gale.cengage.com

**ALL RIGHTS RESERVED.**
No part of this work covered by the copyright herein may be reproduced, transmitted, stored, or used in any form or by any means graphic, electronic, or mechanical, including but not limited to photocopying, recording, scanning, digitizing, taping, Web distribution, information networks, or information storage and retrieval systems, except as permitted under Section 107 or 108 of the 1976 United States Copyright Act, without the prior written permission of the publisher.

For product information and technology assistance, contact us at

Gale Customer Support, 1-800-877-4253
For permission to use material from this text or product, submit all requests online at www.cengage.com/permissions

Further permissions questions can be emailed to permissionrequest@cengage.com

Articles in Greenhaven Press anthologies are often edited for length to meet page requirements. In addition, original titles of these works are changed to clearly present the main thesis and to explicitly indicate the author's opinion. Every effort is made to ensure that Greenhaven Press accurately reflects the original intent of the authors. Every effort has been made to trace the owners of copyrighted material.

Cover Image copyright © Burlingham/Shutterstock.com.

**LIBRARY OF CONGRESS CATALOGING-IN-PUBLICATION DATA**

Gun violence / Noël Merino, book editor.
   pages cm. -- (Opposing viewpoints)
   Includes bibliographical references and index.
   ISBN 978-0-7377-7268-5 (hardcover) -- ISBN 978-0-7377-7269-2 (pbk.)
   1. Gun control--United States. 2. Violent crimes--United States. 3. Firearms and crime--United States. 4. Firearms ownership--Government policy--United States.
I. Merino, Noël.
  HV7436G8762 2015
  364.150973--dc23

                                     2014042036

Printed in Malaysia
1 2 3 4 5 6 7 19 18 17 16 15

# Contents

## Chapter 3: Do Gun Ownership Regulations Reduce Gun Violence?

# Why Consider Opposing Viewpoints?

> "The only way in which a human being can make some approach to knowing the whole of a subject is by hearing what can be said about it by persons of every variety of opinion and studying all modes in which it can be looked at by every character of mind. No wise man ever acquired his wisdom in any mode but this."
>
> *John Stuart Mill*

In our media-intensive culture it is not difficult to find differing opinions. Thousands of newspapers and magazines and dozens of radio and television talk shows resound with differing points of view. The difficulty lies in deciding which opinion to agree with and which "experts" seem the most credible. The more inundated we become with differing opinions and claims, the more essential it is to hone critical reading and thinking skills to evaluate these ideas. Opposing Viewpoints books address this problem directly by presenting stimulating debates that can be used to enhance and teach these skills. The varied opinions contained in each book examine many different aspects of a single issue. While examining these conveniently edited opposing views, readers can develop critical thinking skills such as the ability to compare and contrast authors' credibility, facts, argumentation styles, use of persuasive techniques, and other stylistic tools. In short, the Opposing Viewpoints Series is an ideal way to attain the higher-level thinking and reading skills so essential in a culture of diverse and contradictory opinions.

In addition to providing a tool for critical thinking, Opposing Viewpoints books challenge readers to question their own strongly held opinions and assumptions. Most people form their opinions on the basis of upbringing, peer pressure, and personal, cultural, or professional bias. By reading carefully balanced opposing views, readers must directly confront new ideas as well as the opinions of those with whom they disagree. This is not to argue simplistically that everyone who reads opposing views will—or should—change his or her opinion. Instead, the series enhances readers' understanding of their own views by encouraging confrontation with opposing ideas. Careful examination of others' views can lead to the readers' understanding of the logical inconsistencies in their own opinions, perspective on why they hold an opinion, and the consideration of the possibility that their opinion requires further evaluation.

## Evaluating Other Opinions

To ensure that this type of examination occurs, Opposing Viewpoints books present all types of opinions. Prominent spokespeople on different sides of each issue as well as well-known professionals from many disciplines challenge the reader. An additional goal of the series is to provide a forum for other, less known, or even unpopular viewpoints. The opinion of an ordinary person who has had to make the decision to cut off life support from a terminally ill relative, for example, may be just as valuable and provide just as much insight as a medical ethicist's professional opinion. The editors have two additional purposes in including these less known views. One, the editors encourage readers to respect others' opinions—even when not enhanced by professional credibility. It is only by reading or listening to and objectively evaluating others' ideas that one can determine whether they are worthy of consideration. Two, the inclusion of such viewpoints encourages the important critical thinking skill of objectively evaluating an author's credentials and bias. This evaluation will illuminate an author's reasons for taking a particular stance on an issue and will aid in readers' evaluation of the author's ideas.

It is our hope that these books will give readers a deeper understanding of the issues debated and an appreciation of the complexity of even seemingly simple issues when good and honest people disagree. This awareness is particularly important in a democratic society such as ours in which people enter into public debate to determine the common good. Those with whom one disagrees should not be regarded as enemies but rather as people whose views deserve careful examination and may shed light on one's own.

Thomas Jefferson once said that "difference of opinion leads to inquiry, and inquiry to truth." Jefferson, a broadly educated man, argued that "if a nation expects to be ignorant and free . . . it expects what never was and never will be." As individuals and as a nation, it is imperative that we consider the opinions of others and examine them with skill and discernment. The Opposing Viewpoints series is intended to help readers achieve this goal.

*David L. Bender and Bruno Leone,*
*Founders*

# Introduction

*"Firearm violence accounted for about 70% of all homicides and less than 10% of all nonfatal violent crime from 1993 to 2011."*

*—Michael Planty and
Jennifer L. Truman,
"Firearm Violence, 1993–2011,"
Bureau of Justice Statistics, May 2013*

According to a 2013 report by the Bureau of Justice Statistics within the Office of Justice Programs at the US Department of Justice, in 2011 a total of 478,400 violent crimes were committed with a firearm in the United States. Of these firearm crimes, 11,101—about 2 percent—were homicides. Handguns accounted for about three-quarters of all fatal and nonfatal gun violence in 2011, with other firearms such as shotguns and rifles accounting for the other quarter.

Males are much more likely than females to be the victims of gun homicide. In 2010, 9,340 males were the victims of firearm homicide compared with 1,738 females, for a rate per 100,000 persons of 6.2 for males and 1.1 for females. Similar to gender, race played a role in the likelihood of being the victim of firearm homicide. In 2010, the rate of firearm homicide per 100,000 persons among whites was 1.9, but for black Americans it was 14.6. In addition, age increases the risk of being the victim of firearm homicide: More than half of the victims of gun homicide in 2010 were between the ages of eighteen and thirty-four. Where one lives in the United States also plays a factor: The firearm homicide rate in 2010 per 100,000 persons in the South was 4.4, whereas in the Midwest it was 3.4, in the West 3.0, and in the Northeast 2.8.

The risk of being the victim of nonfatal firearm violence is also affected by gender, race, age, and location. The rate of nonfatal firearm violence per 100,000 persons in 2011 was 190 for males and 160 for females. The rate of nonfatal firearm violence for whites was 140, but for blacks it was 280 and for Hispanics 220. As with firearm homicides, the rate of nonfatal firearm violence is highest for those aged eighteen to thirty-four years old. The rate of nonfatal firearm violence was highest in the South, at 190 incidents per 100,000 persons in 2011, followed by the West at 180, the Midwest at 170, and the Northeast at 130. Throughout the country, the rate of nonfatal firearm violence was highest in urban areas, with a rate of 250, and lowest in rural areas, with a rate of 120. In cities with populations greater than 250,000 people, the rate was between 320 and 460 nonfatal crimes with firearms per 100,000 persons.

Firearms are used in a variety of crimes in the United States. Almost 70 percent of homicides committed in 2011 involved a gun. A little over a quarter of robberies and about 30 percent of aggravated assaults involved guns. Of the 2,218,500 acts of nonfatal firearm violence committed between 2007 and 2011, about half of victim-offender relationships involved strangers. However, 738,000 of victim-offender relationships did not involve strangers. Almost 200,000 were intimates and the rest were friends, relatives, or acquaintances. A little over half a million of these acts of gun violence occurred in the victims' homes or the homes of a friend, neighbor, or relative. Another half million occurred near the victims' homes, and another half million occurred in an open area, street, or on public transportation. The remaining incidents occurred in commercial establishments, parking lots, schools, and other locations.

According to the Bureau of Justice Statistics, of the 2,218,500 acts of nonfatal firearm violence that occurred between 2007 and 2011, only about 23 percent of the victims were injured, with about 16 percent having minor injuries and 7 percent suffering serious injuries. Victims of nonfatal gun violence told the Bureau of Justice Statistics, through its National Crime Victimization Survey, that they only reported violence to the police about half the time. Their reasons for not reporting gun violence incidents to the police were varied: 35 percent said they dealt with the issue another way, 18 percent said the incident was not important enough to call the police, 17 percent who failed to report were concerned that the police could not or would not help, 7 percent feared reprisal if the police were called, and 5 percent did not want to get the offender in trouble. The remaining 18 percent did not cite a most important reason for not reporting an incident of gun violence.

There is a lack of consensus on most of the issues surrounding gun violence in the United States. People fail to agree on the extent of the problem and the methods that should be used to lessen gun violence in America. *Opposing Viewpoints: Gun Violence* seeks to answer the questions "How Serious Is the Problem of Gun Violence?," "What Factors Contribute to Gun Violence?," "Do Gun Ownership Regulations Reduce Gun Violence?," and "What Should Be Done to Reduce Gun Violence?" A wide variety of competing answers to these questions are explored and debated in the chapters that follow.

OPPOSING
VIEWPOINTS®
SERIES

CHAPTER 1

# How Serious Is the Problem of Gun Violence?

# Chapter Preface

The debate about the problem of gun violence in the United States is one that has many viewpoints. Determining the seriousness of the problem involves deciding what level of gun violence is acceptable and what is unacceptable. To a certain extent, assessing the current problem of US gun violence depends to what one compares the current data. Looking at gun violence statistics from foreign countries and examining gun violence statistics from previous years can both be informative.

The United States has less than 5 percent of the world's population, yet it has between a third and a half of the world's civilian-owned guns, according to the Small Arms Survey, an independent research project carried out in Switzerland. The United States has the highest gun ownership rate in the world with over a quarter million civilian firearms—an average of 89 guns per 100 persons. The second-highest gun ownership rate is in Yemen, with 55 guns for every 100 people, followed by Switzerland where there are 46 firearms per 100 people. At the other end of the spectrum, in England there are only 6 guns per 100 persons, in Israel only 7 guns per every 100, and in Jamaica only 8 guns per 100 persons.

Despite having the highest gun ownership rate in the world, the United States does not have the highest rate of firearm homicide. According to a recent report by the United Nations Office on Drugs and Crime, Honduras, Venezuela, Belize, El Salvador, Guatemala, and Jamaica have firearm homicide rates much higher than the United States. Still, the United States is notable among high-income developed countries for having such a high rate. The Organisation for Economic Co-operation and Development reported in 2012 that whereas the United States had a gun homicide rate of 3.2 per

100,000 persons, Canada had a rate of approximately 0.5, Switzerland a rate of 0.8, and the United Kingdom and Israel both had rates of 0.1.

Gun violence peaked in the United States in 1993, when there were 1,547,953 violent crimes committed with a firearm. Eighteen years later in 2011, the Bureau of Justice Statistics reported that the number had dropped to 478,400. In 1993, there were 18,253 firearm homicides, but by 2011 this had dropped by 39 percent to 11,101. Most of the decrease in gun violence occurred between 1993 and 2000. Rates of gun homicide and nonfatal gun violence went up again slightly to a smaller peak in 2006, before coming back down again to present levels. As the commentators in the following chapter illustrate, some believe the drop shows a reduction in the problem of gun violence, whereas others still think the amount of gun violence is far too high.

| "Firearm homicides and suicides are a
continuing public health concern in the
United States."

# Gun Violence in the United States Is a Public Health Concern

*Scott R. Kegler and James A. Mercy*

*In the following viewpoint, Scott R. Kegler and James A. Mercy report that there are tens of thousands of homicides and suicides committed with firearms in the United States each year. The authors say that in recent years, homicide rates in bigger cities have decreased but still remain high, and that suicide rates have increased. Kegler is a member of the Division of Analysis, Research, and Practice Integration and Mercy is a member of the Division of Violence Prevention, both at the US Centers for Disease Control and Prevention's National Center for Injury Prevention and Control.*

Scott R. Kegler and James A. Mercy, "Firearm Homicides and Suicides in Major Metropolitan Areas—United States, 2006–2007 and 2009–2010," *Morbidity and Mortality Weekly Report (MMWR)*, vol. 62, no. 30, August 2, 2013. Centers for Disease Control and Prevention.

As you read, consider the following questions:

1. According to the authors, how many firearm homicides occurred among persons aged ten to nineteen years in 2009–2010?

2. What percentage of firearm suicides are committed by males, according to the authors?

3. According to the authors, suicide rates in the middle-aged population have previously been associated with what?

Firearm homicides and suicides are a continuing public health concern in the United States. During 2009–2010, a total of 22,571 firearm homicides and 38,126 firearm suicides occurred among U.S. residents. This includes 3,397 firearm homicides and 1,548 firearm suicides among persons aged 10–19 years; the firearm homicide rate for this age group was slightly above the all-ages rate. This report updates an earlier report that provided statistics on firearm homicides and suicides in major metropolitan areas for 2006–2007, with special emphasis on persons aged 10–19 years in recognition of the importance of early prevention efforts. Firearm homicide and suicide rates were calculated for the 50 most populous U.S. metropolitan statistical areas (MSAs) for 2009–2010 using mortality data from the National Vital Statistics System (NVSS) and population data from the U.S. Census Bureau. Comparison statistics were recalculated for 2006–2007 to re-flect revisions to MSA delineations and population estimates subsequent to the earlier report. Although the firearm homi-cide rate for large MSAs collectively remained above the na-tional rate during 2009–2010, more than 75% of these MSAs showed a decreased rate from 2006–2007, largely accounting for a national decrease. The firearm homicide rate for persons aged 10–19 years exceeded the all-ages rate in many of these MSAs during 2009–2010, similar to the earlier reporting period. Conversely, although the firearm suicide rate for large MSAs collectively remained below the national rate during 2009–2010, nearly 75% of these MSAs showed an increased rate from 2006–2007, paralleling the national trend. Firearm suicide rates among persons aged 10–19 years were low compared with all-ages rates during both periods. These patterns can inform the development and monitoring of strategies directed at reducing firearm-related violence. . . .

## Firearm Homicide and Suicide Rates

All-ages firearm homicide rates during 2009–2010 varied widely by MSA, ranging from 1.1 to 19.0 per 100,000 residents per year. The rate for all MSAs combined was 4.3, compared with a national rate of 3.7. This represents a decrease from 2006–2007, when the combined MSA rate was 5.2 and the national rate was 4.2. Firearm homicide rates decreased for 78% of MSAs (39 of 50) across reporting periods, accounting for most of the national decrease. The firearm homicide rate among persons aged 10–19 years for the MSAs collectively was 5.1 during 2009–2010. This also reflects a decrease from 2006–2007, when the combined MSA rate for persons aged 10–19 years was 6.6. Rates for this age group exceeded all-ages rates in 72% of MSAs during 2009–2010 (23 of 32 MSAs with reportable youth firearm homicide statistics), comparable to the percentage observed for the earlier period. Males accounted for approximately 85% of firearm homicide victims (all ages) during both reporting periods, for all MSAs combined as well as nationally.

All-ages firearm suicide rates during 2009–2010 also varied widely by MSA, ranging from 1.6 to 11.4. The combined MSA rate was 5.4, compared with a national rate of 7.0. This represents an increase from 2006–2007, when the combined MSA rate was 5.1 and the national rate was 6.5. Across reporting periods, firearm suicide rates increased for 74% of MSAs (37

# Fatal and Nonfatal Firearm Violence in the United States

Individuals use firearms legally for a variety of activities, including recreation, self-protection, and work. However, firearms can also be used to intimidate, coerce, or carry out threats of violence. Fatal and nonfatal firearm violence pose a serious threat to the safety and welfare of the American public. Although violent crime rates have declined in recent years, the U.S. rate of firearm-related deaths is the highest among industrialized countries. In 2010, incidents in the United States involving firearms injured or killed more than 105,000 individuals; there were twice as many nonfatal firearm-related injuries (73,505) than deaths. Nonfatal violence often has significant physical and psychological impacts, including psychological outcomes for those in proximity to individuals who are injured or die from gun violence. The recent, highly publicized, tragic mass shootings in Newtown, Connecticut; Aurora, Colorado; Oak Creek, Wisconsin; and Tucson, Arizona, have sharpened the public's interest in protecting our children and communities from the effects of firearm violence.

*Institute of Medicine (IOM) and National Research Council (NRC), "Priorities for Research to Reduce the Threat of Firearm-Related Violence," 2013.*

of 50), mirroring the national trend. Firearm suicide rates among persons aged 10–19 years were low compared with all-ages rates; the combined MSA rate for this age group was 1.2 during both reporting periods. Males represented approximately 87% of firearm suicides (all ages) in both reporting periods for all MSAs combined and nationally.

During 2009–2010, homicide was the 15th leading cause of death (all ages) in the United States and the second leading cause among persons aged 10–19 years; a firearm injury was the underlying cause in 68% of all homicides and in 83% of homicides among youths. The findings in this report show that despite declining firearm homicide rates in most large metropolitan areas, rates collectively remained higher in these areas compared with the United States overall. Residents of the 50 largest MSAs represented 54% of the U.S. population during 2009–2010 (unchanged from 2006–2007) but accounted for 64% of firearm homicide victims nationally (somewhat below the percentage for 2006–2007). These MSAs accounted for 70% of the national firearm homicide total (2,368 of 3,397) among persons aged 10–19 years.

Concurrently, suicide was the 10th leading cause of death (all ages) nationally and the third leading cause for persons aged 10–19 years; a firearm injury was the underlying cause in 51% of all suicides and in 40% of suicides among youths. Firearm suicide rates increased in most large metropolitan areas across reporting periods; however, rates collectively remained lower in these areas compared with the United States overall. Although residents of the large MSAs comprised more than half of the U.S. population, they accounted for just 42% of firearm suicides nationally (identical to the percentage for 2006–2007). For persons aged 10–19 years, these MSAs accounted for 37% of firearm suicides nationwide. . . .

## Strategies for Reducing Firearm Violence

The observed declines in firearm homicide rates and increases in firearm suicide rates are consistent with longer-term trends in homicide and suicide nationally. Homicide rates generally have been declining in the United States during the past two decades. Factors identified by previous research as influencing this decline include shifting demographics, changes in markets for illegal drugs (e.g., type, demand, and participants), law enforcement responses to gun violence and drug-related crime, increased incarceration rates, community policing and related efforts, and improving economic conditions throughout much of the 1990s. Increasing suicide rates have been prominent in the middle-aged population during the past decade as the percentage of suicides accounted for by this group has steadily increased. Suicide rates within this age group previously have been associated with business cycles; national unemployment rates notably doubled from 2006–2007 to 2009–2010.

A factor likely affecting firearm homicide and suicide is access to firearms by persons at risk for harming themselves or others. Potential strategies for reducing firearm-related violence among such persons include initiatives promoting safe storage of guns, waiting periods to reduce the consequences of impulsive suicidal behavior, designing firearms to make them safer, and efforts such as background checks to prevent high-risk persons from possessing firearms (e.g., persons convicted of violent crimes, persons subject to protective orders because of threats of domestic violence, and persons with documented mental illness posing a risk to themselves or others). Further research is needed to assess the effectiveness of such strategies.

Effective approaches for preventing violence include early education through school-based programs addressing social, emotional, and behavioral competencies; parent and family-based programs promoting positive relationships, communication, support, and proper supervision; and efforts to improve school, neighborhood, and community environments in ways that reduce the likelihood of violence. Promoting the capacity of communities to implement such approaches might prove essential to achieving population-level impacts.

| "*Most Americans are unaware that gun crime is lower today than it was two decades ago.*"

# Gun Violence in the United States Has Declined

***D'Vera Cohn, Paul Taylor, Mark Hugo Lopez, Catherine A. Gallagher, Kim Parker, and Kevin T. Maass***

*In the following viewpoint, D'Vera Cohn, Paul Taylor, Mark Hugo Lopez, Catherine A. Gallagher, Kim Parker, and Kevin T. Maass argue that the rates of gun homicide and other crimes have declined in the past two decades. Nonetheless, they say that the general public is unaware of this decline. The authors report that research has not pinpointed the reasons for the crime decline. Cohn is senior writer, Taylor is executive vice president, Lopez is director of Hispanic research, and Parker is director of the Social & Demographic Trends project, all at the Pew Research Center. Gallagher is director of the Cochrane Collaboration College for Policy at George Mason University, where Maass is a research associate.*

D'Vera Cohn, Paul Taylor, Mark Hugo Lopez, Catherine A. Gallagher, Kim Parker, and Kevin T. Maass, "Gun Homicide Rate Down 49% Since 1993 Peak; Public Unaware," Pew Research Center, May 7, 2013. Copyright © 2013 Pew Research Center. All rights reserved. Reproduced by permission.

As you read, consider the following questions:

1. According to the authors, the firearm homicide rate was how much lower in 2010 than in 1993?

2. Mass shootings—or homicides with more than three victims—accounted for what percentage of homicide deaths from 1980 to 2008, according to a review cited by the authors?

3. The authors contend that one explanation for the decline in crime rates over the past two decades is what historic US Supreme Court decision?

National rates of gun homicide and other violent gun crimes are strikingly lower now than during their peak in the mid-1990s, paralleling a general decline in violent crime, according to a Pew Research Center analysis of government data. Beneath the long-term trend, though, are big differences by decade: Violence plunged through the 1990s, but has declined less dramatically since 2000.

## The Rate of Gun Crime

Compared with 1993, the peak of U.S. gun homicides, the firearm homicide rate was 49% lower in 2010, and there were fewer deaths, even though the nation's population grew. The victimization rate for other violent crimes with a firearm—assaults, robberies and sex crimes—was 75% lower in 2011 than in 1993. Violent nonfatal crime victimization overall (with or without a firearm) also is down markedly (72%) over two decades.

Nearly all the decline in the firearm homicide rate took place in the 1990s; the downward trend stopped in 2001 and resumed slowly in 2007. The victimization rate for other gun crimes plunged in the 1990s, then declined more slowly from 2000 to 2008. The rate appears to be higher in 2011 compared with 2008, but the increase is not statistically significant. Violent nonfatal crime victimization overall also dropped in the 1990s before declining more slowly from 2000 to 2010, then ticked up in 2011.

Despite national attention to the issue of firearm violence, most Americans are unaware that gun crime is lower today than it was two decades ago. According to a new Pew Research Center survey, today 56% of Americans believe gun crime is higher than 20 years ago and only 12% think it is lower.

Looking back 50 years, the U.S. gun homicide rate began rising in the 1960s, surged in the 1970s, and hit peaks in 1980 and the early 1990s. (The number of homicides peaked in the early 1990s.) The plunge in homicides after that meant that firearm homicide rates in the late 2000s were equal to those not seen since the early 1960s. The sharp decline in the U.S. gun homicide rate, combined with a slower decrease in the gun suicide rate, means that gun suicides now account for six in ten firearms deaths, the highest share since at least 1981.

Trends for robberies followed a similar long-term trajectory as homicides, hitting a peak in the early 1990s before declining. . . .

## The Public Interest in Gun Violence

Researchers have studied the decline in firearm crime and violent crime for many years, and though there are theories to explain the decline, there is no consensus among those who study the issue as to why it happened.

There also is debate about the extent of gun ownership in the U.S., although no disagreement that the U.S. has more civilian firearms, both total and per capita, than other nations. Compared with other developed nations, the U.S. has a higher homicide rate and higher rates of gun ownership, but not higher rates for all other crimes.

In the months since the mass shooting at a Newtown, Conn., elementary school in December [2012], the public is paying close attention to the topic of firearms; according to a recent Pew Research Center survey no story received more public attention from mid-March to early April than the debate over gun control. Reducing crime has moved up as a priority for the public in polling this year [2013].

Mass shootings are a matter of great public interest and concern. They also are a relatively small share of shootings overall. According to a Bureau of Justice Statistics review, homicides that claimed at least three lives accounted for less than 1% of all homicide deaths from 1980 to 2008. These homicides, most of which are shootings, increased as a share of all homicides from 0.5% in 1980 to 0.8% in 2008, according to the bureau's data. A Congressional Research Service report, using a definition of four deaths or more, counted 547 deaths from mass shootings in the U.S. from 1983 to 2012.

Looking at the larger topic of firearm deaths, there were 31,672 deaths from guns in the U.S. in 2010. Most (19,392) were suicides; the gun suicide rate has been higher than the gun homicide rate since at least 1981, and the gap is wider than it was in 1981.

## The Public's Knowledge About Crime

Despite the attention to gun violence in recent months, most Americans are unaware that gun crime is markedly lower than it was two decades ago. A new Pew Research Center survey (March 14–17) found that 56% of Americans believe the number of crimes involving a gun is higher than it was 20 years ago; only 12% say it is lower and 26% say it stayed the same. (An additional 6% did not know or did not answer.)

Men (46%) are less likely than women (65%) to say long-term gun crime is up. Young adults, ages 18 to 29, are markedly less likely than other adults to say long-term crime is up—44% do, compared with more than half of other adults. Minority adults are more likely than non-Hispanic whites to say that long-term gun crime is up, 62% compared with 53%.

# Most Americans Unaware of Big Crime Drop Since 1990s

**In recent years, has the number of gun crimes in America gone up, gone down, or stayed the same? (%)**

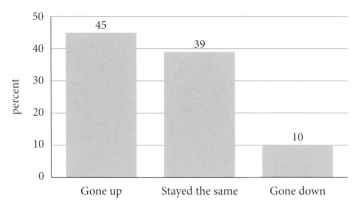

**Compared with 20 years ago, has the number of gun crimes in America gone up, gone down, or stayed the same? (%)**

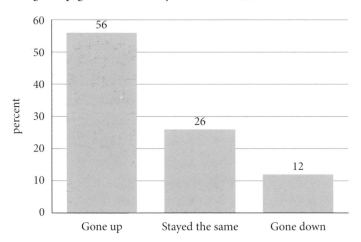

Note: "Don't know/Refused" responses not shown.
Source: Pew Research Center survey, March 14–17, 2013.

TAKEN FROM: D'Vera Cohn et al., "Gun Homicide Rate Down 49% Since 1993 Peak; Public Unaware," Pew Research Center, May 7, 2013.

Asked about trends in the number of gun crimes "in recent years," a plurality of 45% believe the number has gone up, 39% say it is about the same and 10% say it has gone down. (An additional 5% did not know or did not answer.) As with long-term crime, women (57%) are more likely than men (32%) to say that gun crime has increased in recent years. So are nonwhite adults (54%) compared with whites (41%). Adults ages 50 and older (51%) are more likely than those ages 18–49 (42%) to believe gun crime is up.

## The Cause of the Crime Decline

Researchers continue to debate the key factors behind changing crime rates, which is part of a larger discussion about the predictors of crime. There is consensus that demographics played some role: The outsized post–World War II baby boom, which produced a large number of people in the high-crime ages of 15 to 20 in the 1960s and 1970s, helped drive crime up in those years.

A review by the National Academy of Sciences of factors driving recent crime trends cited a decline in rates in the early 1980s as the young boomers got older, then a flare-up by mid-decade in conjunction with a rising street market for crack cocaine, especially in big cities. It noted recruitment of a younger cohort of drug sellers with greater willingness to use guns. By the early 1990s, crack markets withered in part because of lessened demand, and the vibrant national economy made it easier for even low-skilled young people to find jobs rather than get involved in crime.

At the same time, a rising number of people ages 30 and older were incarcerated, due in part to stricter laws, which helped restrain violence among this age group. It is less clear, researchers say, that innovative policing strategies and police crackdowns on use of guns by younger adults played a significant role in reducing crime.

Some researchers have proposed additional explanations as to why crime levels plunged so suddenly, including increased access to abortion and lessened exposure to lead. According to one hypothesis, legalization of abortion after the 1973 Supreme Court *Roe v. Wade* decision resulted in fewer unwanted births, and unwanted children have an increased risk of growing up to become criminals. Another theory links reduced crime to 1970s-era reductions in lead in gasoline; children's exposure to lead causes brain damage that could be associated with violent behavior. The National Academy of Sciences review said it was unlikely that either played a major role, but researchers continue to explore both factors.

## Local Differences Influencing Crime Rates

The plateau in national violent crime rates has raised interest in the topic of how local differences might influence crime levels and trends. Crime reductions took place across the country in the 1990s, but since 2000, patterns have varied more by metropolitan area or city.

One focus of interest is that gun ownership varies widely by region and locality. The National Academy of Sciences review of possible influences on crime trends said there is good evidence of a link between firearm ownership and firearm homicide at the local level; "the causal direction of this relationship remains in dispute, however, with some researchers maintaining that firearm violence elevates rates of gun ownership, but not the reverse."

There is substantial variation within and across regions and localities in a number of other realms, which complicates any attempt to find a single cause for national trends. Among the variations of interest to researchers are policing techniques, punishment policies, culture, economics and residential segregation.

Internationally, a decline in crime, especially property crime, has been documented in many countries since the mid-

1990s. According to the authors of a 30-country study on criminal victimization, there is no general agreement on all the reasons for this decline. They say there is a general consensus that demographic change—specifically, the shrinking proportion of adolescents across Europe—is a common factor causing decreases across Western countries. They also cite wider use of security measures in homes and businesses as a factor in reducing property crime.

But other potential explanations—such as better policing or increased imprisonment—do not apply in Europe, where policies vary widely, the report noted.

| *"Young Americans suffer disproportion- ately from gun violence."*

# Young Guns: How Gun Violence Is Devastating the Millennial Generation

## Chelsea Parsons and Anne Johnson

*In the following viewpoint, Chelsea Parsons and Anne Johnson argue that gun violence in the United States takes a disproportionate toll on young people, both as victims and as perpetrators. The authors claim that the societal impact of youth gun violence includes years of potential life lost and the negative impact of youth criminal conviction. Parsons is vice president of Guns and Crime Policy at the Center for American Progress, and Johnson is the executive director of Generation Progress, the youth division of the Center for American Progress.*

As you read, consider the following questions:

1. What percentage of people murdered with guns in 2010 were under the age of thirty, according to the authors?

Chelsea Parsons and Anne Johnson, "Young Guns: How Gun Violence Is Devastating the Millennial Generation," Center for American Progress, February 2014. Copyright © 2014 Center for American Progress. All rights reserved. Reproduced by permission.

2. According to Parsons and Johnson, how many young people between the ages of ten and twenty-nine were arrested for weapons offenses in 2012?

3. What percentage of people under the age of thirty report having been personally affected or know someone affected by gun violence, according to the authors?

American children and teenagers are 4 times more likely to die by gunfire than their counterparts in Canada, 7 times more likely than young people in Israel, and 65 times more likely to be killed with a gun than children and teenagers in the United Kingdom.[1]

Even though violent crime has steadily declined in recent years—overall violent crime declined 19 percent between 2003 and 2012, and the murder rate declined 17 percent during that period[2]—rates of gun violence remain unacceptably high. On average, 33,000 Americans are killed with guns each year, and the burden of this violence falls disproportionately on young people: 54 percent of people murdered with guns in 2010 were under the age of 30.[3] Young people are also disproportionately the perpetrators of gun violence, as weak gun laws offer easy access to guns in many parts of the country. Far too often, a gun not only takes the life of one young American but also contributes to ruining the life of another young person who pulls the trigger.

And while guns play a role in so many deaths of America's youth, very few public health research dollars are spent to understand the causes of this epidemic and develop policy solutions to address it.[4] In the wake of the tragedy at Sandy Hook Elementary School in December 2012, the issue of gun violence has received renewed attention in this country, and many voices are now calling for solutions to this public health crisis.

In this environment of increased focus on gun violence, millennials' voices are crucial. As discussed in detail below, young Americans suffer disproportionately from gun violence. Beyond the numbers, which are startling, the voices of young people must be heard and the stories told about the effect of this violence on their lives and communities.

In this report, we present data on the disproportionate impact of gun violence on young people; discuss the prevalence of young people as perpetrators of such violence and the ramifications of involvement in the criminal justice system; and highlight poll numbers indicating that millennials are increasingly concerned about the presence of guns in their communities. With an American under the age of 25 dying by gunfire every 70 minutes,[5] we must all recognize that gun violence among youth is an urgent problem that must be addressed.

Every year, about 2.5 million Americans die from all causes, and not surprisingly, very few of them—less than 3 percent—are under the age of 25.[6] But when you consider gun deaths, a different pattern emerges: 21 percent of individuals killed by guns in 2010 were under the age of 25—totaling more than 6,500 deaths.[7]

The third highest cause of death for this age group in 2010 was suicide, and again, guns played a large role, accounting for a plurality—45 percent—of those deaths. In total, guns were the cause of death for 6,201 young people ages 15 to 24 during 2010.[8] This stands in sharp contrast to the risk of gun violence that older individuals face. In 2010, homicide was the 5th leading cause of death for individuals between the ages of 35 and 44; guns accounted for 68 percent of those deaths. Homicide was not even in the top 10 causes of death for individuals ages 45 to 54.[9]

Indeed, gun deaths are not far behind motor vehicle accident deaths: 6,201 young people between the ages of 15 and 24 were killed by guns in 2010, while 7,024 people in this age group were killed in motor vehicle traffic accidents.[10] If current trends continue, gun deaths among this age group are projected to outnumber car accident deaths next year for the first time since 1994.[11]

The problem is not that gun deaths among American youth are going up, but rather that they are failing to go down. While there was a significant decrease in gun deaths among young Americans following the violent crime surge in the late 1980s and early 1990s, in the past decade, gun deaths among young people have barely declined, even as our country continues to make great progress in reducing car accident deaths. In fact, the car accident death rate among people under age 25 is dropping 7 times faster than the gun death rate.[12] Given this trend, gun deaths are on track to surpass motor vehicle traffic deaths for this age group in 2015.

While 13 percent of Americans are black,[13] in 2010, 65 percent of gun murder victims between the ages of 15 and 24 were black. Forty-two percent of the total gun deaths of individuals in this age group were of black males.[14] Young black men in this age group are killed by a gun at a rate that is 4.5 times higher than their white counterparts.[15]

In addition to gun homicides, a large number of young people are victims of nonfatal gun assaults. In 2010, 5,494 individuals in this age range were murdered with a gun,[16] and another 33,519 young people in this category were intentionally shot but survived their injuries.[17]

But looking at the number of gun deaths in the United States only tells part of the story. While the raw number of young people killed by guns is staggering, the impact of gun violence on society is drawn into even sharper relief when considered in terms of years of life lost by gun deaths. This measure considers not just the overall number of deaths attributed to various causes—such as disease, car accidents, and gun violence—but also takes into account the relative age of individuals who died as a result of these causes to provide another measure of the impact on society of each cause of death.[18]

Many diseases cause more deaths each year than gun violence, which could lead one to conclude that the more urgent public health need is to address those causes. But when these causes of death, such as heart disease, cancer, and Alzheimer's disease, are measured in terms of years of potential life lost, their impact on society is reduced compared to gun deaths. The reason for this is simple: Gun violence disproportionately affects young people, who are stricken down decades before individuals who die from other causes. In contrast, life-threatening diseases tend to cause death in individuals who are much older and therefore result in fewer years of potential life lost. Public health researchers have a measure of calculating this pernicious impact of diseases and other causes of death that disproportionately affect the young: years of potential life lost, or YPLL.

More than 1 million years of potential life are lost due to gun deaths each year. These are years of life that young people killed by guns would have achieved educational milestones, entered the workforce, had families, and contributed to the social, economic, and cultural advancement of society in untold ways—all erased by gunfire.

Young people are not only affected by gun violence as victims, young people commit violent gun crimes in high numbers. The easy access youths have to guns across the country creates the opportunity for otherwise nonfatal confrontations between young people to become fatal. This means that incidents that would have ended as simple fistfights or a trip to the hospital end instead with a trip to the morgue. When a young person pulls the trigger, two lives are often changed forever: the victim and the perpetrator. While we rarely devote sustained thought or attention to the impact of gun violence on the individuals who perpetrate these crimes, it is worth considering the effect that involvement in such crimes has on the young people who perpetrate them and on society as a whole.

## Gun Death Rates for Children and Teens

Guns are the second leading cause of death among children and teens ages 1–19 and the number one cause among black children and teens.

- Only motor vehicle accidents kill more children and teens every year.
- White and Asian/Pacific Islander children and teens were nearly three times more likely, American Indian/Alaska Native children and teens more than two times as likely, and Hispanic children and teens one-and-a-half times more likely to be killed in a car accident than by a gun.
- In contrast, black children and teens were twice as likely to be killed by a gun than to be killed in a car accident.

Although total gun deaths dropped in 2010 for the fourth consecutive year, gun death rates remained higher than in the early 1960s.

- In 2010, the rate of gun deaths in children and teens was 30 percent higher than in 1963. . . .
- While black children and teens have experienced the highest rates of gun deaths, the largest number of deaths has been among white children and teens. . . .
- Between 1963 and 2010, 59,265 black children and teens were killed by guns—more than 17 times the recorded lynchings of black people of all ages in the 86 years from 1882 to 1968.

*Children's Defense Fund,*
*"Protect Children, Not Guns 2013," July 24, 2013.*

Young people commit gun offenses in high numbers. In 2012, 75,049 young people between the ages of 10 and 29 were arrested for weapons offenses, such as illegally carrying or possessing a firearm. This group made up 65 percent of all arrests for weapons offenses that year.[19] In 2011, 4,998 individuals between the ages of 12 and 24 were arrested for homicides, and 3,490 of those murders, or 70 percent, involved guns.[20]

Little can compare to the suffering of the family of a gun homicide victim. But it is worth considering the effect of this crime on the perpetrator, as well as the victim, as we all bear the costs of both ends of the equation when it comes to fatal gunfire. A 20-year-old convicted of a gun murder is likely to be sentenced to a long term of incarceration, often life in prison in most federal and state courts[21]—and perhaps appropriately so. But the cost of this imprisonment is staggering: Incarcerating a 20-year-old for life will cost taxpayers roughly $2 million.[22] And this accounts only for the actual costs of incarceration and does not include other costs to society, such as lost productivity and tax revenue, had the 20-year-old avoided a life in prison.

Even nonfatal gun crimes devastatingly affect victims and perpetrators alike. As an initial matter, many juveniles who commit such crimes are treated as adults and prosecuted in the adult criminal justice system. In every state, a person over the age of 17 will be prosecuted as an adult, and in 10 states that age is lowered to 15 or 16.[23] In many states, individuals charged with the most serious offenses, such as murder and attempted murder, will be prosecuted as adults regardless of their age.[24] Once a person is convicted of a serious crime, their life is affected in numerous and often permanent ways.

For those convicted of the most serious crimes, young people face long periods of incarceration in adult correctional facilities.[25] Serving such sentences has a lasting negative impact, even if the offender is eventually released. Young offenders will often be housed in adult prisons, where they are commingled with adult offenders and face a heightened risk of assault and suicide.[26] Many facilities do not offer adequate educational and rehabilitation programs for young offenders, and the facilities are often located far from the offenders' families, making it difficult to maintain a connection to family and friends.[27]

The effects of felony conviction on young people that fall short of long-term incarceration are no less devastating. In many states, individuals convicted of felonies are denied the opportunity to participate in some of the basic functions of citizenship, such as the right to vote and jury service. A felony conviction is also a frequent barrier to employment, housing, public assistance, and student loans.[28]

This generation of young Americans is losing far too many of its members to gun violence, both as victims and as perpetrators. The young people who are convicted of serious felony offenses and receive long terms of incarceration as the result of bad decisions that are exacerbated by easy access to guns represent a significant loss to society. Just as the years of potential life lost because of gun death is a drain on society, so is the potential extinguished or dimmed by involvement in the criminal justice system.

Young people are not ignorant about the toll of gun violence on their generation. Indeed, young people today choose to own guns in much lower numbers than their counterparts in previous generations. Data from the General Social Survey, a public-opinion survey conducted every two years, found that household gun-ownership rates among people under age 30 fell to 23 percent in 2012. This is down from a high of 47 percent in the 1970s and well below the overall household gun-ownership rate of 34 percent.[29]

Additionally, millennials are now increasingly expressing concern about gun violence. A 2013 poll commissioned by the Center for American Progress, Generation Progress, and Mayors Against Illegal Guns found that 70 percent of respondents under the age of 30 agreed that "the gun culture in our society has gotten out of control," and 52 percent said that they feel safer in communities with fewer guns.[30]

Part of this concern about guns may come from personal experience with gun violence. Remarkably, 30 percent of people under the age of 30 reported having been personally affected or knowing someone who has been affected by gun violence, and 60 percent expressed concern that gun violence may personally affect them or their communities in the future.[31] These numbers were even higher among young African Americans, Latinos, and Asian Americans: Collectively, 73 percent of respondents from those racial and ethnic groups reported being worried about being personally affected by gun violence in the future.[32]

These views about and experiences with the gun culture in the United States by younger Americans have translated to high levels of support for specific policies intended to reduce gun violence and keep guns out of the hands of dangerous people. The 2013 poll found that while the proposal to require background checks for all gun sales is supported by the vast majority of Americans over the age of 30—86 percent said they supported such a law—this policy is even more popular among Americans aged 18 to 29, with 92 percent saying they supported this measure.[33]

The United States pays a high price for its incredibly high rates of gun violence—by one measure, roughly $174 billion in 2010 alone.[34] But even more important is the cost of this violence in terms of lives lost and communities devastated. Right now there are roughly 21 million high-school-aged teenagers in the United States between the ages of 14 and 18.[35] If current trends continue, in the next year, nearly 1,700 of them will be killed by guns, and more than 17,000 people in this age group will die because of gunfire in the next 10 years.[36]

# Endnotes

1. Children's Defense Fund, "Protect Children Not Guns 2013" (2013), p. 33, available at http://www.childrensdefense.org/child-research-data-publications/data/protect-children-not-guns-2013.pdf.

2. Federal Bureau of Investigation, "Crime in the United States 2012, Table 1A: Percent Change in Volume and Rate per 100,000 Inhabitants for 2 years, 5 years, and 10 years," available at http://www.fbi.gov/about-us/cjis/ucr/crime-in-the-u.s/2012/crime-in-the-u.s.-2012/tables/1tabledatadecoverviewpdf/table_1_crime_in_the_united_states_by_volume_and_rate_per_100000_inhabitants_1993-2012.xls (last accessed February 2014).

3. Centers for Disease Control and Prevention, "WISQARS: Fatal Injury Data," available at http://www.cdc.gov/injury/wisqars/fatal.html (last accessed February 2014).

4. Mayors Against Illegal Guns, "Access Denied: How the Gun Lobby Is Depriving Police, Policy Makers, and the Public of the Data We Need to Prevent Gun Violence" (2013), p. 12, available at http://libcloud.s3.amazonaws.com/9/cc/3/1482/AccessDenied_print_021713.pdf.

5. Centers for Disease Control and Prevention, "WISQARS: Fatal Injury Data."

6. Centers for Disease Control and Prevention, National Center for Health Statistics, "Underlying Cause of Death 1999–2010," available at http://wonder.cdc.gov/ucd-icd10.html (last accessed February 2014).

7. Centers for Disease Control and Prevention, "WISQARS: Fatal Injury Data."

8. Centers for Disease Control and Prevention, "10 Leading Causes of Death by Age Group, United States–2010" (2011), available at http://www.cdc.gov/injury/wisqars/pdf/10LCID_All_Deaths_By_Age_Group_2010-a.pdf.

9. Ibid.

10. Centers for Disease Control and Prevention, "WISQARS: Fatal Injury Data."

11. Ibid. The comparison of gun deaths versus car accident deaths differs when you consider all age groups, rather than just young people. While gun deaths among people under age 25 briefly exceeded motor vehicle traffic deaths for three years during the high-crime era of the early 1990s, when considering the entire U.S. population, car accident deaths have exceeded gun deaths since at least 1950. Garen J. Wintemute, "Responding to the Crisis of Firearm Violence in the United States," JAMA Internal Medicine 173 (9) (2013), available at http://archinte.jamanetwork.com/article.aspx?articleid=1661391. Gun deaths are projected to exceed car deaths among the general population in 2015 as well. Chris Christoff and Ilan Kolet, "American Gun Deaths to Exceed Traffic Fatalities by 2015," Bloomberg News, December 19, 2012, available at http://www.bloomberg.com/news/2012-12-19/american-gun-deaths-to-exceed-traffic-fatalities-by-2015.html.

12. Centers for Disease Control and Prevention, "WISQARS: Fatal Injury Data."

13. U.S. Bureau of the Census, "USA People QuickFacts," available at http://quickfacts.census.gov/qfd/states/00000.html (last accessed February 2014).

14. Centers for Disease Control and Prevention, "WISQARS: Fatal Injury Data."

15. Ibid.

16. Ibid.

17. Centers for Disease Control and Prevention, "WISQARS: Nonfatal Injury Data," available at http://www.cdc.gov/injury/wisqars/nonfatal.html (last accessed February 2014).

18. Rhode Island Public Health Association, "Rhode Island Public Health Brief, Years of Productive Life Lost" (2011), available at http://www.ripha.org/content/ripha/Data_Briefs/Data_Brie_YPLL_FIN.pdf.

19. Federal Bureau of Investigation, "Uniform Crime Reports: Arrests," available at http://www.fbi.gov/about-us/cjis/ucr/crime-in-the-u.s/2012/crime-in-the-u.s.-2012/tables/38tabledatadecoverviewpdf (last accessed February 2014).

20. C. Puzzanchera, G. Chamberlin, and W. Kang, "Easy Access to the FBI's Supplementary Homicide Reports: 1980–2011, Year of incident by age of offender for United States" (2012), available at http://ojjdp.gov/ojstatbb/ezashr/asp/off_display.asp.

21. For a discussion of common sentencing practices in murder cases, see Findlaw, "First Degree Murder Penalties and Sentencing," available at http://criminal.findlaw.com/criminal-charges/first-degree-murder-penalties-and-sentencing.html (last accessed February 2014).

22. Ashley Nellis, "The Lives of Juvenile Lifers: Findings from a National Survey" (Washington: The Sentencing Project, 2012), p. 33, available at http://sentencingproject.org/doc/publications/jj_The_Lives_of_Juvenile_Lifers.pdf.

23. Anne Teigen, "Juvenile Age of Jurisdiction and Transfer to Adult Court Laws," National Conference of State Legislatures, January 10, 2014, available at http://www.ncsl.org/research/civil-and-criminal-justice/juvenile-age-of-jurisdiction-and-transfer-to-adult-court-laws.aspx.

24. Ibid.

25. Nellis, "The Lives of Juvenile Lifers," p. 19. In *Graham v. Florida*, 560 U.S. 48 (2010), the Supreme Court held that individuals cannot be sentenced to life without parole for non-homicide offenses committed when they were juveniles. While this ruling helps ensure that many juvenile offenders are not subject to lifetime incarceration, many young people who commit serious crimes, including gun crimes, continue to face long terms of imprisonment.

26. Nellis, "The Lives of Juvenile Lifers," p. 19.

27. Ibid., pp. 23–25.

28. For information about the collateral consequences of criminal convictions, see The Sentencing Project, "Collateral Consequences Publications," available at http://www.sentencingproject.org/template/page.cfm?id=141 (last accessed February 2014).

29. Sabrina Tavernise and Robert Gebeloff, "Share of Homes with Guns Shows 4-Decade Decline," *The New York Times*, March 9, 2013, available at http://www.nytimes.com/2013/03/10/us/rate-of-gun-ownership-is-down-survey-shows.html?pagewanted=all&_r=0.

30. GBA Strategies and Chesapeake Beach Consulting, "Millennials Say Gun Culture Has Gotten Out of Control" (2013), available at http://www.americanprogress.org/wp-content/uploads/2013/04/Natlguns13m1-041613.pdf.

31. Ibid.

32. Ibid.

33. Ibid.

34. Children's Safety Network, "The Cost of Firearm Violence," available at http://www.childrenssafetynetwork.org/cost-gun-violence (last accessed February 2014).

35. U.S. Bureau of the Census, "Annual Estimates of the Resident Population by Sex, Single Year of Age, Race, and Hispanic Origin for the United States: April 1, 2010 to July 1, 2012," available at http://factfinder2.census.gov/faces/tableservices/jsf/pages/productview.xhtml?pid=PEP_2012_PEPALL6N&prodType=table (last accessed February 2014).

36. Centers for Disease Control and Prevention, "WISQARS: Fatal Injury Data."

> "Politicians . . . have been more than
> happy to ignore the easily identifiable,
> but politically tricky, origins of gang
> violence and criminal activity."

# There Is a Problem with Politics, Not Guns, in the United States

## Michael Schaus

*In the following viewpoint, Michael Schaus argues that Chicago's high rate of gun violence coupled with strict gun control illustrates that the problem there is not about guns. Schaus contends that rather than being a problem of guns, the real problem in Chicago is the ruling politics of the last several years. He claims that progressive, liberal politics created a situation that led to gang violence and criminal activity. Schaus is the associate editor for* Townhall Finance *and the executive producer for Ransom Notes Radio.*

As you read, consider the following questions:

1. Schaus claims that it is not too little gun control but a failure of what that has brought Chicago to a state of deterioration?

Michael Schaus, "Guns Don't Cause Gang Violence—Democrats Do," *Townhall*, May 5, 2014. Copyright © 2014 Michael Schaus. All rights reserved. Reproduced by permission.

2. The author claims that it is unsurprising that Chicago has a violence problem due to what two factors?

3. What political party does Schaus claim has had a monopoly on Chicago government for many years?

Between Friday night, and Sunday evening [May 2–4, 2014], 28 people had been shot in Rahm Emanuel's gun control utopia (Chicago). Which, unbelievably, shows an improvement over the previous weekend, which tacked on more than 40 gunshot victims to the city's climbing statistics. And, heck, with the CPD's [Chicago Police Department's] recent scandal surrounding how they classify various crimes, it almost makes you wonder if these numbers are more "ballpark" figures than actual stats.

## Gun Control in Chicago

It would be easy to begin writing an article aimed at the abject failure of gun control. But, truthfully, Chicago's failure goes far deeper than misguided (Bloomberg approved) regulation schemes. Since the days of [former Chicago mayor] Bill Thompson came to an end (nearly 80 years ago) the Democrats have had a monopoly on efforts to fix violence, gang activity, and inequality in the Windy City. And if you're thinking, "It doesn't seem to be working". . . well, you'd be right.

Even Chicago's police superintendent seems to understand this (to an extent). Of course, being the good Progressive that he is, he glossed right over the primary culprits for Chicago's woes and instead focused on disarming the law-abiding citizens he has sworn to protect. Via WGN radio:

> It's going to take a while to fix poverty and the breakup of the family unit, and education and jobs. But we can do something about gun laws today and we're just not doing it.

Right . . . because *that's* the problem with Chicago: Too little gun control. I mean, heck, it hasn't exactly worked out that well so far, but why not double down? Right? The fact is, the failure of *Liberalism* has brought the city to its current state of deterioration. The Chicago model of unconstitutional restrictions on keeping and bearing arms has done little more than add fuel to the fire. Politicians, meanwhile, have been more than happy to ignore the easily identifiable, but politically tricky, origins of gang violence and criminal activity.

## The Real Cause of Violence

Despite embracing the union-led concept of public education, nearly 80 percent of the city's 8th graders aren't proficient in reading and writing. And while schools are going without heat, electricity, or (in some cases) adequate security, teachers make a salary that is more than $10,000 *higher* than the median Chicago *household's* income. Being one of the best-funded education systems in America, it borders on audacious absurdity when the unions start crying about not having enough resources. Especially when you consider the way Democrats are on course to spend the city into being the next Detroit.

Of course, all that tax revenue and debt was being used for a good cause, right? Wasn't that deficit spending, borrowing, and begging from the state and federal government (as well as the general public) supposed to help fund antipoverty programs, and create "shovel ready" jobs? Because, if that *was* the case, it seems kinda curious that Chicago has some uncomfortably high poverty rates when compared to other large US cities. This almost seems like a silly thing to ask, but: *Hey Democrats, maybe we could try something new?*

With an education system that has utterly failed inner-city youth, and antipoverty programs that have done little more than spur an exodus of private capital, it's unsurprising to see violence sweep areas of Chicago like an epidemic . . . especially when the "Progressives" downtown have managed to disarm most of the remaining *law-abiding* citizens.

## The Failure of Progressivism

The lesson of Chicago is rather simple: Progressivism can't provide for the poor. Progressivism can't provide the masses with quality education, health care, or housing. And, Progressivism can't keep its people safe. While Democrats have taxed, spent, and regulated with relative impunity, Chicago continues to suffer misery and inequality on scales rarely matched by other US cities.

Chicago Democrat politicians continue to repackage, and resell, to the city's voters the very policy proposals that helped create their current plight. I often say that Progressives haven't had a new idea in roughly 100 years (seriously: health care, tax hikes, deficit spending . . . it's all been tried), and Chicago is a prime example of Progressive monopoly in government. Each new administration promised its citizens the same policies as the previous administration, with "new and improved" projected results.

The only thing closer to [Albert] Einstein's definition of insanity was America's decision to elect a politician from that city to be president of the United States . . . Twice.

| "In the fourteen months since the mass shooting in Newtown, CT, there have been at least 44 school shootings."

# There Is an Epidemic of School Shootings

**Moms Demand Action for Gun Sense in America and Mayors Against Illegal Guns**

*In the following viewpoint, Moms Demand Action for Gun Sense in America and Mayors Against Illegal Guns claim that for a fourteen-month period from December 2012 to February 2014, there were forty-four US school shootings resulting in deaths and injuries. The authors contend that the school shootings often stem from a school confrontation, and young people get the guns from family members. Moms Demand Action and Mayors Against Illegal Guns focus on enacting gun reforms through their blanket organization, Everytown for Gun Safety.*

As you read, consider the following questions:

1. Approximately what fraction of school shootings during the time period discussed by the authors did the shooting result in at least one fatality?

"Analysis of School Shootings: December 15, 2012–February 10, 2014," Moms Demand Action for Gun Sense in America and Mayors Against Illegal Guns, February 12, 2014. Copyright © 2014 Everytown for Gun Safety Support Fund. All rights reserved. Reproduced by permission.

2. According to the authors, approximately what fraction of the school shootings occurred after a confrontation?

3. During the fourteen-month period the authors discuss, approximately how many school shootings a month occurred at K–12 schools?

In the fourteen months since [December 2012–February 2014] the mass shooting in Newtown, CT, there have been at least 44 school shootings, including fatal and nonfatal assaults, suicides, and unintentional shootings—an average of more than three a month.

In the first six weeks of 2014 alone, there were 13 school shootings, including one eight-day period in which there were four shootings in K–12 schools.

## An Epidemic of School Shootings

These school shootings resulted in 28 deaths and 37 nonfatal gunshot injuries. In 49 percent of these incidents, at least one person died.

Of the K–12 school shootings in which the shooter's age was known, 70 percent (20 of 28 incidents) were perpetrated by minors. Among those shootings where it was possible to determine the source of the firearm, three-quarters of the shooters obtained their guns from home.

In 16 cases—more than a third of all incidents—at least one person was shot after a school yard argument or confrontation escalated and a gun was at hand.

The shooters ranged from 5 to 53 years of age.

The 44 school shootings occurred in 24 states across the country. Sixty-four percent of the shootings took place at K–12 schools and thirty-six percent took place on college or university campuses.

Thirty-three shootings (75 percent) involved an assault or homicide; of these, 12 incidents resulted in at least one homi-

cide. In 11 incidents, the shooter attempted or completed suicide—in 4 incidents after shooting someone else. In 4 other
incidents, no one was injured.

## School Confrontations Lead to Shootings

At least 16 of the shootings—more than a third of total incidents—occurred after a confrontation between students inten-
sified and shots were fired. Among the shootings that occurred after an altercation escalated:

- *January 9, 2014, Liberty Technology Magnet High School,
  Jackson, Tennessee.* Two male students, ages 16 and 17,
  got into a disagreement over a female student. After
  classes were dismissed, the two boys got into a fight,
  and one student shot the other in the thigh.

- *January 30, 2014, Eastern Florida State College, Palm
  Bay, Florida.* A verbal argument between students escalated into a fight in the parking lot of the main academic building, and a 24-year-old student pulled a
  handgun from his car and shot another student in the
  chest.

- *August 23, 2013, North Panola High School, Sardis, Mississippi.* A 15-year-old was killed by a single gunshot to
  the chest after a fight broke out at a high school foot-
  ball game. Three people involved in the fight were arrested for the shooting, including a 17-year old.

- *January 16, 2013, Chicago State University, Chicago, Illinois.* After a basketball game between two rival high
  schools at Chicago State University, a fight erupted during the post-game handshake and a 17-year-old high
  school student was fatally shot.

- *January 22, 2013, Lone Star College, Houston, Texas.* A
  confrontation that began when two young men
  bumped into each other in the doorway of an academic
  building ended when one fired at least 10 shots. Three

## School Shootings: December 15, 2012–February 10, 2014

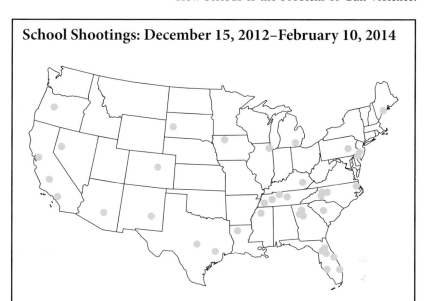

TAKEN FROM: Moms Demand Action for Gun Sense in America and Mayors Against Illegal Guns, "Analysis of School Shootings: December 15, 2012–February 10, 2014," February 12, 2014.

people were wounded, including two students and a 55-year-old maintenance worker who was shot in the leg.

- *April 15, 2013, Grambling State University, Grambling, Louisiana.* Three students, ages 19 to 21, were treated for gunshot wounds after a fight broke out outside a school dormitory.

- *December 4, 2013, West Orange High School, Winter Garden, Florida.* A 17-year-old student shot a 15-year-old classmate during a fight that began as classes were being dismissed.

## The Source of the Guns

An average of two school shootings took place at K–12 schools each month between December 15, 2012, and February 10, 2014.

Among shootings at K–12 schools in which the shooter's age was known, 70 percent (14 of 20 incidents) were perpetrated by minors.

Many of the students who perpetrated these shootings had easy access to guns at home. In several cases, investigators declined to comment on how the child obtained a firearm because the incidents are under active investigation. But in the eight incidents where the source of the firearm was known, three-quarters of the shooters used a gun they obtained from home. This includes three cases where a minor used a gun to attempt or complete suicide in his school.

The incidents included the following:

- *January 10, 2013, Taft Union High School, Taft, California.* Sixteen-year-old Bryan Oliver walked into his science classroom with a 12-gauge Winchester shotgun that belonged to his brother, aimed at a 16-year-old classmate he said had bullied him, and fired a single shot that struck the boy in the chest. Bryan fired one more shot, but no one else was harmed.

- *March 21, 2013, Davidson Middle School, Southgate, Michigan.* Just before classes started one morning, 13-year-old Tyler Nichols walked into the bathroom at his school, pulled out a handgun, and committed suicide. Police reported that the gun was legally owned by a family member but had not been safely secured.

- *April 29, 2013, La Salle High School, Cincinnati, Ohio.* Joseph Poynter, age 17, was sitting at his desk in a computer lab with about two dozen other students at just after 9:00 a.m. one morning when he pulled out a .45-caliber semiautomatic handgun and fired a single shot at his head. Joseph had acquired the gun from home, where it was ordinarily stored in a safe.

- *October 21, 2013, Sparks Middle School, Sparks, Nevada.* Shouting "Why are you laughing at me? Why are you doing this to me?," 12-year-old Jose Reyes fatally shot a teacher and wounded two 12-year-old students with a 9mm semiautomatic Ruger handgun. His parents told investigators that the gun had been stored in a case on a shelf above the refrigerator. The case was not locked.

- *January 14, 2014, Berrendo Middle School, Roswell, New Mexico.* During cold or inclement weather, students at Berrendo Middle School gather in the school gymnasium to wait for school to start. They were there one morning when Mason Campbell, age 12, walked into the gym and pulled out a 20-gauge shotgun that he'd taken from home. The boy opened fire on his fellow students, critically wounding an 11-year-old boy, seriously injuring a 13-year-old girl, and slightly wounding an adult staff member. After Mason fired all three rounds in the gun, a teacher stepped forward and persuaded him to put it down.

> "With an average of 300 shootings every day, it should be no surprise that a few of them occur in or near schools."

# Gun Violence Is Decreasing and School Shootings Are Rare

*Dewey G. Cornell*

*In the following viewpoint, Dewey G. Cornell argues that although every mass shooting causes the public to seek a quick fix, it is important to remain objective about the scope of the problem. Cornell claims that gun violence has decreased, school shootings are not common, mental illness is not the problem, and gun violence prevention is more complicated than enacting laws or imprisoning people. Cornell is Bunker Professor of Education in the Curry School of Education at the University of Virginia and director of its Virginia Youth Violence Project.*

As you read, consider the following questions:

1. According to the author, approximately how many deaths from guns occur every day in the United States?

Dewey G. Cornell, "Gun Violence and Mass Shootings—Myths, Facts, and Solutions," *Washington Post*, June 11, 2014. Copyright © 2014 Dewey G. Cornell. All rights reserved. Reproduced by permission.

2. According to Cornell, the United States has a gun homicide rate that is seven times higher than the rate in each of what eleven countries?

3. The author claims that it is a mistake to believe that we must be able to do what in order to prevent violence?

After every horrific shooting, it is human nature to search for clues that might explain what happened, and how to keep it from happening again. Unfortunately, every case offers a few promising leads that seem to be contradicted by the next case. In the 1990s, we had city shootings that generated concern about the stress of "urban war zones," followed by rural school shootings attributed to the pressures on boys raised in small towns. The 1999 shooting at suburban Columbine High School convinced many people that the underlying problem was bullying.

Last year [2013], Adam Lanza's [2012] attack of Sandy Hook Elementary School aroused concern about school safety and inspired calls to place armed guards in elementary schools. Santa Barbara shooter Elliot Rodger was interviewed by law enforcement officers who mistakenly concluded that he was not dangerous, prompting nationwide calls for better police training.

## The Problem of Gun Violence

If we have learned anything, it should be that there is no simple solution to the problem of mass shootings and that we should be wary of quick-fix ideas. It is time to step back and look more objectively at the larger patterns and trends.

*1. Yes, gun violence is ubiquitous in the United States.*

According to data from the Centers for Disease Control and Prevention, there are approximately 81,300 nonfatal injuries and 31,672 deaths every year involving guns. That works out to about 308 shootings and 86 deaths every day. The cases we hear about in the news are highly selective and not representative.

*2. But gun violence is not increasing.*

We often see reports claiming that gun violence is increasing, but national trends show otherwise. FBI [Federal Bureau of Investigation] crime statistics show that gun violence was far higher 20 years ago. A few extra cases in a short time frame are likely to be chance fluctuations or copycat effects.

*3. School shootings are statistically rare.*

With an average of 300 shootings every day, it should be no surprise that a few of them occur in or near schools. According to FBI crime statistics, most homicides, including most multi-victim homicides, occur in homes, not schools. There are more mass shootings in restaurants than in schools, but no one has called for waitpersons to carry guns. Children are almost 100 times more likely to be murdered outside of school than at school, which makes massive expenditures for school-building security seem like a misallocation of tax dollars.

*4. Gun violence is not due to mental illness.*

It seems intuitive that anyone who commits a mass shooting must be mentally ill, but this is a misuse of the term "mental illness." Mental illness is a term reserved for the most severe mental disorders where the person has severe symptoms such as delusions or hallucinations. Decades of mental health research show that only a small proportion of persons with mental illness commit violent acts, and together they account for only a fraction of violent crime. Some mass shooters have had a mental illness. Most do not.

*5. Gun violence could be further reduced.*

Almost every modern nation in the world has far lower rates of gun violence than the U.S. For example, gun homicides are seven times higher in the U.S. than in Australia, Canada, France, Germany, India, Italy, Japan, South Korea,

Spain, Sweden, and the United Kingdom. Other democratic nations with gun safety laws do not experience our levels of gun violence.

But the political debate over gun rights has made it appear impossible to regulate firearms without sacrificing the Second Amendment. And the connection between guns and violence is not as simple as "guns cause crime" or "guns make us safer." There is scientific evidence, however, that some policies, such as restricting high-risk individuals (such as felons and spouse abusers) from access to firearms, will reduce (but not eliminate) rates of violent crime.

*6. Prevention does not require prediction.*

There is a mistaken belief that we must be able to predict violence in order to prevent it. On the contrary, we can prevent problems without prediction if we take a public health approach. Public health programs have dramatically reduced lung cancer by preventing smoking. Automobile accidents are curtailed by traffic regulations, safer cars, and driver training. Real violence prevention cannot wait until there is a gunman at the door but must start before problems escalate into violence. For example, there are numerous controlled studies demonstrating that school-based counseling and violence prevention programs are effective at teaching students how to resolve conflicts and problems without resorting to violence. Prevention must begin early to be most effective.

*7. Locking people up is not the answer.*

We need a sea change in our approach to threats of violence. The police are hamstrung by an antiquated model which requires them to either arrest someone for a crime or determine that they are mentally ill and imminently about to harm someone. Most cases do not fit into either pigeonhole. Locking people up in a jail or a hospital to prevent violence is not the answer.

In case after case of mass shootings, we learn later that family members, friends, and even mental health professionals were concerned that someone needed help. Predicting violence is difficult, but identifying that someone needs assistance is not so difficult. This is where we need to readjust our focus and concentrate on helping people in distress. This approach requires not only a change in police policy but also community mental health services that are oriented around prevention.

Although we will never eliminate violence, effective prevention programs can do much to reduce its prevalence. We do not read in the news media about the people who threatened violence but were helped. Prevention is invisible to the public when it succeeds. In fact, there have been many successful cases, and we have likely prevented far more shootings than have occurred. We need more widespread use of a threat-assessment approach in which we investigate threats more carefully and provide help for persons who are so distressed that they are threatening violence. We need mental health services more focused on anger and alienation, in addition to the traditional problems of anxiety and depression.

Finally, we need to improve the quality as well as the quantity of mental health services and focus on helping the larger population of people in distress rather than those fitting a narrow definition of mental illness.

# Periodical and Internet Sources Bibliography

*The following articles have been selected to supplement the diverse views presented in this chapter.*

| | |
|---|---|
| Doug Bandow | "Gun Rights and Liberty Go Hand in Hand," *Investor's Business Daily*, February 22, 2013. |
| Trevor Burrus | "Face It: Guns Are Here to Stay," *New York Daily News*, January 7, 2013. |
| Nora Caplan-Bricker | "Are Guns a Public Health Issue? Let Us Count the Ways . . ." *New Republic*, April 3, 2014. |
| Daniel Greenfield | "America Doesn't Have a Gun Problem, It Has a Gang Problem," FrontPageMag.com, December 31, 2012. |
| David Kopel | "Guns in America: Arming the Right People Can Save Lives," *Los Angeles Times*, January 15, 2013. |
| John Lott | "Children and Guns: The Fear and the Reality," *National Review Online*, May 13, 2013. |
| Dean Obeidallah | "Gun Violence Is a Public Health Epidemic," CNN, November 8, 2013. |
| David Paulin | "Second Amendment Culture Wars: Eastern Elites vs. Gun-Friendly Red States," *American Thinker*, March 13, 2011. |
| Rob Waters | "Gun Violence: The Public Health Issue Politicians Want to Ignore," *Forbes*, July 24, 2012. |
| Kyle Wintersteen | "10 Need-to-Know Gun Control Myths," *Guns & Ammo*, May 1, 2013. |

OPPOSING
VIEWPOINTS®
SERIES

CHAPTER 2

# What Factors Contribute to Gun Violence?

# Chapter Preface

Americans are divided in opinion about the causes of gun violence. Factors cited as relevant vary widely, from blaming the availability of guns to the breakdown of the family. Identifying the factors that contribute to gun violence is important, since being able to address the issue of gun violence depends upon knowing where to focus public policy.

A 2013 poll by CNN, *Time* magazine, and ORC International found the public divided on the reasons for gun violence. When asked to give their opinion on the primary cause of gun violence from a list of three choices, 37 percent blamed influences of popular culture, 37 percent blamed the way parents raise their children, 23 percent blamed the availability of guns, and 3 percent had no opinion.

Respondents to polls on the causes of gun violence are, of course, limited by the options given by the pollsters. A 2013 poll by Gallup asked Americans about the factors to blame for mass shootings. Respondents could pick multiple factors in this poll from a list provided by Gallup. In this poll, 48 percent said that the failure of the mental health system to identify individuals who are a danger to others was to blame a great deal, and another 32 percent said it was to blame a fair amount. Many respondents also blamed easy access to guns, with 40 percent finding such easy access a great deal to blame for mass shootings and 21 percent a fair amount to blame. Thirty-seven percent thought drug use was a great deal to blame, and 29 percent believed drug use a fair amount to blame for shootings. Thirty-two percent blamed violence in movies, video games, and music lyrics a great deal, and 24 percent believed a fair amount. Sixty percent of Americans—split evenly on blaming a great deal or a fair amount—thought that the spread of extremist viewpoints on the Internet was a contributing factor to shootings, and the same amount identified insufficient security at public buildings as a factor.

A 2013 poll of American law enforcement by PoliceOne .com found similar diversity of opinion. When asked to identify the biggest cause of gun violence in the United States, 38 percent of law enforcement identified a decline in parenting and family values as the key factor. Fifteen percent blamed parole, early release, and short sentencing for violent offenders. Fourteen percent blamed pop culture influence from violent movies and video games. Ten percent thought that poor identification and treatment of mentally ill individuals was to blame. Only 4 percent of law enforcement said that the cause of gun violence in America was the prevalence of guns and the ease of obtaining them.

Just like the variation in the polls mentioned above, the authors of the viewpoints in the following chapter illustrate that there is a wide diversity of opinion on the causes of gun violence in the United States. There may, in fact, be multiple causes, and successfully addressing the issue of gun violence depends upon accurately identifying the key contributing factors.

> "When it comes to the right to bear arms, the Land of the Free is in a league of its own."

# America's Exceptional Gun Culture

### Elias Groll

*In the following viewpoint, Elias Groll argues that the United States is one of a handful of countries that has a constitutional right to bear arms. Additionally, Groll cites figures showing that the United States has more guns than any other nation and the highest rate of gun ownership in the world. He claims that, as a result, the United States also has high rates of firearm-related suicide and homicide, which he says undermines any theory that high gun ownership reduces gun violence. Groll is an editorial assistant at* Foreign Policy.

As you read, consider the following questions:

1. The author cites a survey that found that there are approximately how many small arms owned by civilians in the United States?

Elias Groll, "America's Exceptional Gun Culture," *Foreign Policy*, December 19, 2012. Copyright © 2012 Foreign Policy. All rights reserved. Reproduced by permission.

2. According to Groll, the firearm-related homicide rate for five- to fourteen-year-olds in the United States is how much higher than the rate of other industrialized nations?

3. In what US Supreme Court case was the Second Amendment most recently interpreted to support an *individual* right to firearms, according to Groll?

Though the issue has been largely on the political back burner for the last four years, last week's tragedy in Newtown, Connecticut, has already prompted a new push for gun control laws by the Obama administration and congressional Democrats. The president suggested in his speech in Newtown on Sunday that he would use "whatever power this office holds" to prevent similar events from happening in the future, and White House spokesman Jay Carney said on Tuesday that the White House would consider supporting congressional proposals for "common sense gun control measures like the assault weapons ban." (Even the National Rifle Association has pledged to make "meaningful contributions to help make sure this never happens again.")

Such a push is likely to meet stiff resistance from Second Amendment advocates. But even if it passed, the United States would still be a major outlier when it comes to gun ownership and culture. As the following facts and figures from around the world make clear, when it comes to the right to bear arms, the Land of the Free is in a league of its own.

## The Stockpile of Civilian-Owned Guns in the United States Dwarfs All Other Countries

According to the 2007 Small Arms Survey—the best, most recent study of the number of guns available in the world—civilians in the United States own roughly 270 million small arms, which is more than the next 17 countries combined (the runner-up on the list is India, with 46 million firearms). The rate of ownership in the United States—90 firearms per 100 people—is also the world's highest (again the runner-up, Yemen, is a distant second with 60 firearms per 100 people). The report notes that there are around 650 million civilian-owned firearms in the entire world, which means more than 40 percent of these are in the United States, and that about 4.5 million out of the roughly 8 million new firearms manufactured annually are purchased in the United States. Keep in mind that the United States represents less than five percent of the world's population.

## "Children in Other Industrialized Nations Are Not Dying from Guns"

Gun violence is killing and injuring American children at an astoundingly high rate. In the United States, only car crashes and cancer claim the lives of more children between the ages of 5 and 14 than firearms, according to a 2002 study that appeared in the *Journal of Trauma: Injury, Infection, and Critical Care*. "Children in other industrialized nations are not dying from guns," the authors wrote. "Compared with children 5–14 years old in other industrialized nations, the firearm-related homicide rate in the United States is 17 times higher, the firearm-related suicide rate 10 times higher, and the unintentional firearm-related death rate 9 times higher. Overall, before a child in the United States reaches 15 years of age, he or she is 5 times more likely than a child in the rest of the industrialized world to be murdered, 2 times as likely to commit suicide and 12 times more likely to die a firearm-related death."

The investigators also found a clear link between elevated levels of guns and child mortality rates across U.S. states, suggesting that more guns lead to more child deaths not only across international borders but also across the United States. Critically, the authors concluded that children living in states

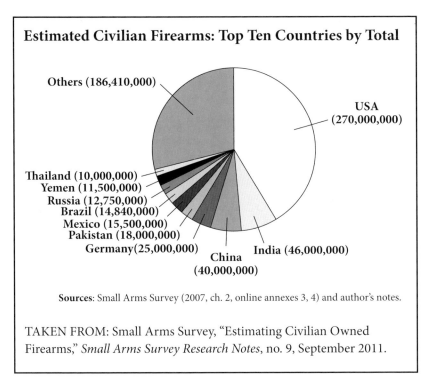

**Estimated Civilian Firearms: Top Ten Countries by Total**

Others (186,410,000)

USA (270,000,000)

Thailand (10,000,000)
Yemen (11,500,000)
Russia (12,750,000)
Brazil (14,840,000)
Mexico (15,500,000)
Pakistan (18,000,000)
Germany (25,000,000)

China (40,000,000)

India (46,000,000)

Sources: Small Arms Survey (2007, ch. 2, online annexes 3, 4) and author's notes.

TAKEN FROM: Small Arms Survey, "Estimating Civilian Owned Firearms," *Small Arms Survey Research Notes*, no. 9, September 2011.

with large numbers of guns were *not* more likely to be victims of violence or suicide that did not involve firearms. Instead, the presence of guns makes possible a kind of violence that few young people could inflict on themselves or one another otherwise.

## The United States Is the Gun-Related Murder Capital of the Developed World

In no other developed country do as many people die in gun-related homicides than in the United States. According to statistics compiled by the United Nations, 3.2 out of 100,000 Americans were killed by guns in 2010. As a frame of reference, consider that Japan, a country with one of the world's most notorious mafias, the *yakuza*, has virtually eliminated gun-related homicides.

Of all the countries in the world, Honduras has the highest gun-related homicide rate, with 68.4 deaths for every

100,000 people. But Honduras, like its fellow Latin American countries Colombia (27.1 gun-related deaths for every 100,000 people) and Mexico (10 per 100,000 people), has been engaged in a brutal drug war against well-funded and well-armed cartels and gangs. These factors are not at play in the United States, which is vastly richer and has a significantly more effective state apparatus.

## The United States Is Nearly Alone in Enshrining Gun Rights in Its Constitution (Sort of)

The Second Amendment of the U.S. Constitution, in full, reads: "A well-regulated militia, being necessary to the security of a free state, the right of the people to keep and bear arms, shall not be infringed." Over time, this amendment has been interpreted as guaranteeing individuals the right to possess a wide variety of firearms and, in many cases, to be able to carry those guns concealed on one's person or openly in a hip holster. U.S. courts have repeatedly upheld that interpretation, most recently in the 2008 case *District of Columbia v. Heller*. In a 5–4 ruling, the justices struck down Washington, D.C.'s ban on handguns and rejected the notion that the Second Amendment permits individual gun ownership only for those participating in a "well-regulated militia."

It is important to note that critics of the *Heller* ruling argue that it applies a distorted reading of the Second Amendment that deliberately removes the text from the context of its drafting. Many historians claim that the amendment was drafted in response to British efforts to disarm unhappy colonists, and that the maintenance of private arms was seen as an integral part of preserving the ability to muster a militia. In this reading, the Second Amendment does not protect the individual right to bear arms.

The *Heller* ruling places the United States within a decidedly small club of nations—alongside Guatemala, Haiti, and

Mexico—that guarantee the right to bear arms in their constitutions. According to the United Nations, these countries also experience relatively high rates of firearm-related homicides. While data is unavailable for Haiti, the United States and Mexico both saw around 10,000 gun deaths in 2010, while Guatemala, a significantly smaller country with only 15 million people, witnessed 5,000 gun deaths. If easy access to guns is supposed to guarantee safety and reduce gun violence, the experiences of these countries simply don't support that theory.

"America's unique level of gun violence
... is partially the expected outcome of
immoral and ineffective government
policies."

# The Drug War Is a Cause of Inner-City Gun Violence

### Trevor Burrus

*In the following viewpoint, Trevor Burrus argues that the frequently purported causes of gun violence are usually mistaken and not based on scientific research. Burrus claims that two of the contributing causes to gun violence are actually government programs: the drug war and the public education system. Burrus contends that the prohibition on drugs has created a war zone in inner-city (often minority) neighborhoods, where gun violence is common and guns ubiquitous. In addition, he says that the inadequate education system keeps these youths trapped in a cycle of criminal activity. Burrus is a research fellow at the Cato Institute.*

As you read, consider the following questions:

1. According to Burrus, how many guns are there in the United States?

Trevor Burrus, "How Shameful Policies Increase America's Gun Violence," *Huffington Post*, January 30, 2013. Copyright © 2013 Trevor Burrus. All rights reserved. Reproduced by permission.

2. The United States has an incarceration rate that is how much higher than any other developed country, according to the author?

3. According to the author, the gun murder rate in the United States is how many times greater than the average for other developed countries?

This week [January 30, 2013], a Senate Judiciary Committee hearing asks the question, "what should America do about gun violence?" As usual, the primary focus is on guns rather than those who misuse them, but unfortunately both President [Barack] Obama's and Sen. Dianne Feinstein's proposals will do little to keep guns out of the hands of criminals. There are 300 million guns in America, and, without a politically impossible and undesirable program of mass confiscation, it will continue to be quite easy for wrongdoers to get weapons in America. Perhaps, instead of trying to extract a thimbleful of water from that ocean of weapons, we should shift our focus to why so many Americans want to harm each other.

## The Explanation for America's Gun Violence

Studies of gun violence often use a compare-and-contrast methodology to find variables between nations that may explain a difference in violent crime rates. Many of the proposed causes for America's uniquely violent culture—from video games to taking God out of schools—have little scientific backing and seem like irrelevant squabbles over tastes and preferences. Yet government programs that do real, measurable harm to our citizens and predictably push them toward gun violence are too often overlooked.

First and foremost is the oppressive and ineffective drug war that has destroyed inner-city neighborhoods and severely

## The Drug War and Gun Violence

Legal bans on drug sales lead to a vacuum in legal regulation; instead of going to court, drug suppliers settle their disputes by shooting each other. Meanwhile, interdiction efforts raise the price of drugs by curbing supply, making local drug supply monopolies (i.e., gang turf) a rich prize to be fought over.

*Noah Smith, "The Single Best Anti-Gun-Death Policy?*
*Ending the Drug War,"* Atlantic, *December 21, 2012.*

harmed the life prospects of millions of Americans, most acutely, young, African-American men.

As Prohibition-era America showed, banning a highly in-demand substance increases the violence surrounding that substance. When legal methods cannot be used to settle contract and other disputes, extra-legal methods (i.e., the point of a gun) will be used. Moreover, unsavory characters will tend to traffic the prohibited substances, further escalating violent business practices. These new businessmen also facilitate the illegal gun trade, brazenly ignoring assault weapons bans and other cosmetic limits on gun ownership. Those guns then flood the black market, giving easy access to would-be criminals and mass shooters. A 2001 Justice Department study found that 20 percent of prison inmates received their guns from a drug dealer or off the street. Comparatively, only 0.7 percent of the weapons were obtained at gun shows. Which "loophole" should we be focusing on closing?

## The Two Causes of Gun Violence

Caught in the middle of this is the American citizen, particularly young, black males, who often grow up in inner cities that have more in common with war zones than suburban neighborhoods. The U.S. government's "solution" to this problem has been mass incarceration on a level rarely seen in world history; with a prison rate currently six to 10 times the rate of any other developed country. In many American inner cities where the drug war is most earnestly waged, up to 80 percent of young African-American males have criminal records. These young men will endure a lifetime of legalized discrimination and difficulty finding employment, often because they simply chose to put a prohibited substance into their own bodies.

The devastation wreaked by these policies upon the African-American community is astounding. A robust sense of community—a sense of belonging, a sense of responsibility for your fellow citizens—is one of the best modifiers for interpersonal violence. Yet, for decades the American government's policies have been systematically destroying families and communities, mostly African-American, through an immoral and endless drug war.

As if to dig the knife deeper in the wound, the government offers the children living in these communities a "way out" in the form of a moribund and pitiful public school system. Students are quite literally trapped in their local, geographically designated school, and parents who try to rescue their children from gang-ridden schools by manipulating their legal place of residence can be sent to prison. As a virtual monopoly, the ineffective schools lack sufficient incentives to adequately serve students.

The grossly inadequate education system, coupled with the drug war, is a devastating one-two punch. If the U.S. government were trying to destroy inner-city communities and diminish the life prospects of millions of people, it could hardly do better than hit them with this destructive pincer maneuver. Similarly, the government could scarcely improve its strategy if it were trying to systematically increase gun violence in America over the course of 50 years.

## An Expected Outcome

Left with few avenues to better their situation, inner-city children increasingly turn to the drug trade and other types of criminal activities that offer better immediate futures than staying in useless schools, and then often find themselves caught by the war on drugs. Generations of inner-city children are denied meaningful avenues to better themselves and have few role models to look up to.

America's unique level of gun violence is not something to scratch our heads at as if it is a bolt from the blue—it is partially the expected outcome of immoral and ineffective government policies.

Tragedies like Sandy Hook [referring to the school shooting at Sandy Hook Elementary School in Newtown, Connecticut] cause us to hold a mirror up to our society, and when it comes to gun violence in America, we don't like what we see. The gun murder rate in America is 20 times the average for developed countries, and we react to this with a mixture of confusion and shame. Yet some causes of America's violent culture are not so confusing, although they are certainly shameful.

| *"We know how to reduce urban violence:*
*data-driven, proactive policing."*

# The Guns of Chicago: And the Safe Sidewalks of New York

*Heather Mac Donald*

*In the following viewpoint, Heather Mac Donald argues that many of the government responses to gun violence are misguided because most urban gun violence is caused by juveniles who have family problems. Mac Donald claims that more spending on antipoverty programs and more gun control initiatives are not solutions to urban shootings. Rather, the author contends that proactive policing results in juveniles leaving guns at home and lowers gun violence rates. Mac Donald is the Thomas W. Smith Fellow at the Manhattan Institute for Policy Research and a contributing editor to* City Journal.

As you read, consider the following questions:

1. According to the author, how much money has the Department of Education given to so-called Promise Neighborhoods since 2010?

Heather Mac Donald, "The Guns of Chicago: And the Safe Sidewalks of New York," *Weekly Standard*, vol. 18, no. 24, March 4, 2013. Copyright © 2013 Weekly Standard. All rights reserved. Reproduced by permission.

2. How does Mac Donald describe the victims and perpe-trators of urban shootings?

3. Mac Donald claims that how many homicides of minor-ity victims have been averted since the 1990s due to New York's proactive policing?

President Barack Obama recently went to Chicago to pro-mote his poverty and gun violence initiatives and actually spoke a good deal of truth. "There's no more important ingre-dient for success, nothing that would be more important for us reducing violence than strong, stable families, which means we should do more to promote marriage and encourage fa-therhood," he said. Reiterating a line from his State of the Union speech, he observed: "What makes you a man is not the ability to make a child; it's the courage to raise one." And though he paid the obligatory tribute to single mothers, he added with remarkable candor: "I wish I had had a father who was around and involved."

What Obama didn't say also came as a relief. In the worst of all possible worlds, he could have trotted out hackneyed poverty and racism themes from the academy—that biased law enforcement and an "epidemic" of incarceration, for ex-ample, are harming what would otherwise be law-abiding inner-city communities. Unfortunately, the president's depu-ties are pursuing policies informed by such ideas behind the scenes, but at least Obama is not putting the power of the presidential bully pulpit behind them.

Had Obama left it at that, he would have made an impor-tant contribution to public discourse. But though he rightly recognized the distinction between civil society and govern-ment ("When a child opens fire on another child, there is a hole in that child's heart that government can't fill"), he came to Chicago bristling with big government programs that threaten to cancel out his personal responsibility theme. The administration is promoting an initiative called "Promise

Zones," based on a concept that has been endlessly flogged by liberal foundations: that if we can just form "collaboratives" to coordinate the existing morass of taxpayer-funded social service agencies and programs, we will achieve a breakthrough in the self-defeating behaviors that cause poverty today. The Ford Foundation's Gray Areas program in New Haven in the 1960s was a progenitor of this idea (and the seedbed for the War on Poverty); more recently the Annie E. Casey Foundation's New Futures collaborative bombed spectacularly.

Paradoxically, streamlining social service delivery requires adding yet more agencies to the existing mix: The Promise Zones project will involve, inter alia, the U.S. Departments of Justice, Treasury, Commerce, Agriculture, Health and Human Services, Education, and Housing and Urban Development. Cecilia Muñoz, director of the White House Domestic Policy Council, explained the Promise Zones idea to the *New York Times*: "The premise behind this is that the federal government has to be a positive actor in all of this effort—but as an actor who's a partner." Got that? A "partner," not just an "actor."

Actually, Promise Zones are not even new to the Obama administration. Since 2010, the Department of Education has doled out nearly $100 million to "Promise Neighborhoods" (almost the same thing as Promise Zones) in over 50 cities. Not surprisingly, the administration is mum about the results.

The Promise Zones will also give out tax and regulatory breaks to encourage businesses to locate in distressed areas. While it is always gratifying to see liberals acknowledge, however fleetingly, that lower taxes and less onerous regulations are good for economic activity, lower taxes alone do not overcome the disincentive to locate a business in a crime-plagued area.

Obama's other announced antipoverty initiatives—such as raising the minimum wage and providing universal preschool education—are progressive evergreens whose efficacy is deeply contested, to say the least. But the biggest disappointment in the president's agenda is his unwillingness to move the debate on gun violence beyond the stale polarities of gun control and gun rights. The fact that he chose Chicago as the site for his speech was a tip-off that he would be breaking no new ground.

Though this latest eruption of the gun control–gun rights standoff was triggered by that rarest of all events—an in-school massacre by a non-student—the public discourse on gun violence has subtly shifted since the Newtown tragedy to acknowledge (however sotto voce) that the real problem lies elsewhere. An event as thankfully rare as the Newtown massacre is impossible to predict and nearly as difficult to prevent. Both sides in the gun debate have nevertheless seized upon it to promote their favorite cause—whether banning assault weapons or arming everyone to the teeth. The most common gun violence, by contrast, is drearily predictable and, unlike mass shootings, the source of thousands of homicides a year. It occurs overwhelmingly in certain locations of cities—over the past 30 years in Boston, for example, 75 percent of the city's shootings occurred in 4.5 percent of its area, whereas 88.5 percent of the city's street segments experienced not a single shooting. Urban shootings are retaliatory or the product of the most trivial of slights. They are committed with handguns, not assault rifles. And both victims and perpetrators come disproportionately from fatherless homes and communities and are disproportionately minority, by huge margins. Reforming the involuntary commitment laws and beefing up mental health services are largely irrelevant; though the shooters have serious problems with impulse control and are clearly a danger to themselves and others, few would be deemed mentally ill.

While it is unclear how to prevent mass shootings—short of the unlikely event of removing all guns from the public—we know how to reduce urban violence: data-driven, proactive policing. The New York City Police Department has brought crime and homicide down an unmatched 80 percent since the early 1990s by deploying officers to locations where crime patterns are emerging, encouraging them to use their lawful discretion to question people about suspicious behavior, enforcing quality-of-life laws, and holding police commanders accountable for crime on their watch.

Gun control has had only a limited effect on inner-city violence, as the case of Chicago demonstrates. Despite the Windy City's strict firearms bans, juveniles under the age of 17 are killed there four times as often as youth in New York. In 2012, Chicago logged 506 homicides; New York, with three times the population, tallied 418. The difference lies largely in policing. Chicago has historically eschewed proactive policing, and is for that reason still embraced by the left—however incredibly—as a model for law enforcement. Some South Side community leaders, however, know better and are calling for the reconstitution of antigang units just so their officers can stop and question more suspects on the streets.

Whereas Chicago's minority neighborhoods are awash in illegal guns, criminals in New York report leaving their guns at home or stashing them in communal locations to avoid being stopped with a gun on their person. As a result, 10,000 homicides of minority victims have been averted since the early 1990s. And by lowering violence and fear, proactive policing has done more to revitalize poor neighborhoods than billions of dollars of government-funded social programs have ever accomplished.

President Obama should have gone to New York City, rather than Chicago, for his poverty and gun violence speech. If he amplified his marriage and fatherhood message and spread the word about how policing can save lives, he could in fact be the transformative president that his followers believe him to be.

*"Innumerable studies have found a correlation between severe mental illness and violent behavior."*

# Mental Illness Has Proven Itself a Risk Factor for Gun Violence

*Ann Coulter*

*In the following viewpoint, Ann Coulter argues that when mentally disturbed people commit violent murders, there are often warning signs. Coulter contends that in these cases, it is currently too difficult to get a person involuntarily committed, even though doing so could prevent mass shootings. Coulter claims that initiatives that make it harder for mentally stable people to get guns put the focus on the wrong class of people. Coulter is a syndicated columnist, lawyer, and author of several books, including* Demonic: How the Liberal Mob Is Endangering America.

As you read, consider the following questions:

1. According to Coulter, why was Virginia Tech prohibited from being told about shooter Seung-Hui Cho's mental health problems?

Ann Coulter, "Guns Don't Kill People, the Mentally Ill Do," January 16, 2013. Copyright 2013 Ann Coulter, Distributed by Universal UClick. Copyright © 2013 Ann Coulter. All rights reserved. Reproduced by permission.

2. It is estimated that what approximate percentage range of all homicides committed by disturbed individuals occur during their first psychotic episode, according to the author?

3. Coulter claims that whenever a psychopath commits a shocking murder in the United States, the knee-jerk reaction is to do what?

Seung-Hui Cho, who committed the Virginia Tech [Virginia Polytechnic Institute and State University] massacre in 2007, had been diagnosed with severe anxiety disorder as a child and placed under treatment.

But Virginia Tech was prohibited from being told about Cho's mental health problems because of federal privacy laws.

At college, Cho engaged in behavior even more bizarre than the average college student. He stalked three women and, at one point, went totally silent, refusing to speak even to his roommates. He was involuntarily committed to a mental institution for one night and then unaccountably unleashed on the public, whereupon he proceeded to engage in the deadliest mass shooting by an individual in U.S. history.

## A Number of Warning Signs

The 2011 Tucson, Ariz., shopping mall shooter, Jared Loughner, was so obviously disturbed that if he'd stayed in Pima Community College long enough to make the yearbook, he would have been named "Most Likely to Commit Mass Murder."

After Loughner got a tattoo, the artist, Carl Grace, remarked: "That's a weird dude. That's a Columbine candidate."

One of Loughner's teachers, Ben McGahee, filed numerous complaints against him, hoping to have him removed from class. "When I turned my back to write on the board," McGahee said, "I would always turn back quickly—to see if he had a gun."

On her first day at school, student Lynda Sorensen emailed her friends about Loughner: "We do have one student in the class who was disruptive today, I'm not certain yet if he was on drugs (as one person surmised) or disturbed. He scares me a bit. The teacher tried to throw him out and he refused to go, so I talked to the teacher afterward. Hopefully he will be out of class very soon, and not come back with an automatic weapon."

The last of several emails Sorensen sent about Loughner said: "We have a mentally unstable person in the class that scares the living cr** out of me. He is one of those whose picture you see on the news, after he has come into class with an automatic weapon. Everyone interviewed would say, Yeah, he was in my math class and he was really weird."

That was the summer before Loughner killed six people at the Tucson shopping mall, including a federal judge and a 9-year-old girl, and critically wounded Rep. Gabrielle Giffords, among others.

Loughner also had run-ins with the law, including one charge for possessing drug paraphernalia—a lethal combination with mental illness. He was eventually asked to leave college on mental health grounds, released on the public without warning.

Perhaps if Carl Grace, Ben McGahee or Lynda Sorensen worked in the mental health field, six people wouldn't have had to die that January morning in Tucson. But committing Loughner to a mental institution in Arizona would have required a court order stating that he was a danger to himself and others.

## The Connection Between Mental Illness and Violence

Innumerable studies have found a correlation between severe mental illness and violent behavior. Thirty-one to 61 percent of all homicides committed by disturbed individuals occur

# A Reasonable Curtailment of Rights

A therapist is allowed to alert the authorities if and when a patient is a harm to himself or others. The police could then arrest that patient, if need be, and place him or her in psychiatric care. I've never heard anyone argue that this is not a reasonable curtailment of rights and liberties.

We broadly agree on this principle.

That being the case, shouldn't we also broadly agree that denying this person access to firearms, a much lesser curtailment of their right and liberties, makes perfect sense?

*Dennis Scimeca,*
*"I'm Mentally Ill, and I Should Never Own a Gun,"*
Daily Dot, *June 3, 2014.*

during their first psychotic episode—which is why mass murderers often have no criminal record. There's no time to wait with the mentally ill.

James Holmes, the accused Aurora, Colo., shooter, was under psychiatric care at the University of Colorado long before he shot up a movie theater. According to news reports and court filings, Holmes told his psychiatrist, Dr. Lynne Fenton, that he fantasized about killing "a lot of people," but she refused law enforcement's offer to place Holmes under confinement for 72 hours.

However, Fenton did drop Holmes as a patient after he made threats against another school psychiatrist. And after Holmes made threats against a professor, he was asked to leave campus. But he wasn't committed. People who knew he was deeply troubled just pushed him onto society to cause havoc elsewhere.

Little is known so far about Adam Lanza, the alleged New-town, Conn., elementary school shooter, but anyone who could shoot a terrified child and say to himself, "That was fun—I think I'll do it 20 more times!" is not all there.

It has been reported that Lanza's mother, his first victim, was trying to have him involuntarily committed to a mental institution, triggering his rage. If true—and the media seem remarkably uninterested in finding out if it is true—Mrs. Lanza would have had to undergo a long and grueling process, unlikely to succeed.

As the *New York Times*' Joe Nocera recently wrote: "Connecticut's laws are so restrictive in terms of the proof required to get someone committed that Adam Lanza's mother would probably not have been able to get him help even if she had tried."

## The Wrong Approach

Taking guns away from single women who live alone and other law-abiding citizens without mental illnesses will do nothing about the Chos, Loughners, Holmeses or Lanzas. Such people have to be separated from civil society, for the public's sake as well as their own. But this is nearly impossible because the ACLU [American Civil Liberties Union] has decided that being psychotic is a civil right.

Consequently, whenever a psychopath with a million gigantic warning signs commits a shocking murder, the knee-jerk reaction is to place yet more controls on guns. By now, guns are the most heavily regulated product in America.

It hasn't worked.

Even if it could work—and it can't—there are still subway tracks, machetes, fists and bombs. The most deadly massacre at a school in U.S. history was at an elementary school in Michigan in 1927. It was committed with a bomb. By a mentally disturbed man.

How about trying something new for once?

> "In the context of gun violence, those with mental illness have become easy scapegoats."

# Guns—Not the Mentally Ill—Kill People

## Abby Rapoport

*In the following viewpoint, Abby Rapoport argues that recent proposed legislation to reduce gun violence by keeping guns away from the mentally ill is misguided. Rapoport claims that the legislation could have the effect of discouraging mentally ill individuals from seeking treatment, where such treatment is actually the best way to prevent violence. Additionally, Rapoport claims the legislation conveys the message that mentally ill people are dangerous, when, in fact, they are actually more likely to be victims of violence than to perpetrate it. Rapoport is a staff writer for the* American Prospect.

As you read, consider the following questions:

1. According to Rapoport, which national organization is leading the charge to blame gun violence on the mentally ill?

Abby Rapoport, "Guns—Not the Mentally Ill—Kill People," *American Prospect*, February 7, 2013. Copyright © 2013 American Prospect. All rights reserved. Reproduced by permission.

2. The author says that following in the footsteps of New York, what eight states are also considering gun control measures aimed at the mentally ill?

3. Rapoport claims that what percentage of violent crime is committed by those with mental illness?

After a year of violent tragedies that culminated with the elementary school shooting in Newtown, Connecticut, America is finally having a conversation about gun control. For the many who want to decrease access to firearms in the wake of several mass shootings, new laws being proposed around the country to limit and regulate guns and ammunition represent a momentous first step.

But running through the gun control debate is a more delicate conversation: how to handle mental health treatment in America. Among both Democrats and Republicans, in both the pro-gun and anti-gun lobbies, there's a widespread belief that mental health treatment and monitoring is key to decreasing gun violence. Shining more light on the needs and struggles of the mentally ill would normally be a positive change; mental health programs and services have been cut year after year in the name of austerity. But in the context of gun violence, those with mental illness have become easy scapegoats. Rather than offering solutions to the existing problems that patients and providers face, policy makers instead promise to keep guns out of the hands of the mentally ill. The trouble is, that often means presenting policies that are actually detrimental to mental health treatment—threatening doctor-patient confidentiality, expanding forced treatment rather than successful voluntary programs, and further stigmatizing people with databases that track who's been committed to hospitals or mental institutions.

The National Rifle Association has led the charge to blame those with mental illness. "The truth is that our society is populated by an unknown number of genuine monsters—

people so deranged, so evil, so possessed by voices and driven by demons that no sane person can possibly ever comprehend them," NRA executive vice president Wayne LaPierre said at his December 21 press conference. "How can we possibly even guess how many, given our nation's refusal to create an active national database of the mentally ill?" Ann Coulter was more succinct: "Guns don't kill people—the mentally ill do."

It's not just the NRA and the right wing who are turning mentally ill Americans into political pawns. See, for instance, New York's new gun control law, the first passed after Newtown. In addition to banning assault weapons and semiautomatic guns with military-level components, the legislation requires therapists, nurses and other mental health care providers to alert state health authorities if they deem a patient is a danger to self or others. That would then allow the state to confiscate the person's guns. The measure broadens the confiscation powers to include those who voluntarily seek commitment to a mental health facility—in other words, the people who get help without being forced. Finally, it strengthens Kendra's Law, which allows the courts to involuntarily commit the mentally ill.

Other states will very likely follow suit. Legislatures in Ohio and Colorado will both consider measures to make it easier to commit people. Maryland governor Martin O'Malley wants to broaden the range of people banned from owning guns to include those who have been civilly committed to mental institutions at any time. Policy makers in Louisiana, Massachusetts, Pennsylvania, Rhode Island, and Utah have also proposed measures aimed specifically at keeping the mentally ill from getting guns.

The new rules and proposals perpetuate the assumption that people with mental illness are dangerous; instead of making people safer, the requirements may hurt efforts to get the mentally ill treatment. For instance, the expanded reporting requirements mean mental health providers must alert officials if a patient may harm herself or others. Law enforcement officials can then show up and confiscate any guns the patient owns. Mental health providers are already supposed to report if a patient seems in imminent danger of doing harm, but the new law broadens that rule. It could easily chip away trust between therapists and their patients. The threat of gun confiscation may make it less likely that folks like policemen and veterans suffering from trauma get help, since many are gun owners. "It's very hard to get people to come forward and get help," says Ron Honberg, the national director for policy and legal affairs at the mental health advocacy group National Alliance on Mental Illness. "If they're aware that by seeking help they're going to lose their right to have a gun, we're concerned it's going to have a chilling effect."

It's also not likely to slow down the violence. Predicting murderous behavior is extremely difficult and most of the time, the providers can't do it accurately. "We're making an assumption that violence can be predicted," Honberg says. In fact, it's *lack* of treatment, combined with substance abuse and a history of violence, that tend to be the best predictors of future violence. Yet many of New York's new laws—like the reporting requirements and the push to put more mentally ill people in government databases—target those who are already getting help.

The issue is not that mental health advocates want to arm more people but that those with mental illness are being singled out by often well-intended gun control measures, which could increase the stigma around getting help. By focusing on keeping guns out of the hands of the mentally ill specifically—and not those who have histories of substance abuse, domestic violence, and other predictors of violent behavior—these laws perpetuate the idea that the mentally ill are an overwhelming threat. So does a recent report from Mayors Against Illegal Guns, which highlights the gaps in re-

## The Risk Factors for a Mass Shooting

On the face of it, a mass shooting is the product of a disordered mental process. You don't have to be a psychiatrist: What normal person would go out and shoot a bunch of strangers?

But the risk factors for a mass shooting are shared by a lot of people who aren't going to do it. If you paint the picture of a young, isolated, delusional young man—that probably describes thousands of other young men.

A 2001 study looked specifically at 34 adolescent mass murderers, all male. 70 percent were described as a loner. 61.5 percent had problems with substance abuse. 48 percent had preoccupations with weapons. 43.5 percent had been victims of bullying. Only 23 percent had a documented psychiatric history of any kind—which means 3 out of 4 did not.

*Jeffrey Swanson, interviewed by Lois Beckett, "Myth vs. Fact: Violence and Mental Health," ProPublica, June 10, 2014.*

porting mentally ill people to the NICS [National Instant Criminal Background Check System] database; in red pullout text, it prominently displays examples of mentally ill people responsible for violence.

The stereotype that the mentally ill are very violent is simply incorrect. According to the National Institute of Mental Health, people with severe mental illness, like schizophrenia, are up to three times more likely to be violent, but "most people with [severe mental illness] are not violent and most violent acts are not committed by people with [severe mental illness]." On the whole, those with mental illness are responsible for only 5 percent of violent crimes.

"People with mental illness are so much more likely to be victims of crimes than perpetrators that it's almost immeasurable," says Debbie Plotnick, the senior director of state policy at Mental Health America, an advocacy group for mental health treatment. According to one study, people with mental illness are 11 times more likely to be the victims of violence.

Fortunately, the national conversation hasn't been entirely negative. Advocates see an undeniable opportunity to get more funding and attention to mental health services. For the first time in recent memory, governors and lawmakers across the political spectrum are pushing for more dollars to help those with mental illness. That's particularly important because over the past four years, $4.35 billion was cut in funding for Medicaid mental health funding, substance abuse, housing, and other mental health programs at the state and federal level. Now, even Kansas's ultraconservative governor Sam Brownback is pushing for $10 million more for mental health care. South Carolina governor Nikki Haley, a Tea Party favorite, has also argued for an increase in funding. In Oklahoma, Colorado, Minnesota, and Missouri, legislatures will very likely consider investing more heavily in treatment of mental illness.

The investment is badly needed. Over the years, most states have cut back to only providing emergency and crisis care for mental illnesses. That's both expensive and ineffective. Harvey Rosenthal, executive director of the New York Association of Psychiatric Rehabilitation Services, says the most successful programs are those that focus on getting a patient help wherever they are, while providing other necessities like housing. For instance, the "housing first" model provides housing to people who might not otherwise qualify and then layers on services like mental health and substance abuse treatment. Such programs, like New York's Pathways to Housing, have an astounding 85 percent retention rate, and according to Rosenthal, they're successful because they tailor to a person's specific needs rather than telling patients, "You're mentally ill and you need medicine."

More attention to the cracks in care for the mentally ill is a good thing. While it may not have much to do with gun violence, there *is* a serious mental health care problem in the country.

# Periodical and Internet Sources Bibliography

*The following articles have been selected to supplement the diverse views presented in this chapter.*

| | |
|---|---|
| Ted Galen Carpenter | "Don't Blame American Guns for Mexico's Drug War," *National Interest*, August 14, 2013. |
| Erick Erickson | "The Real Gun Violence Problem," RedState .com, January 9, 2013. |
| Todd Essig | "The Myth of Mental Illness and Gun Violence," *Forbes*, June 28, 2014. |
| Carl E. Fisher and Jeffrey A. Lieberman | "Getting the Facts Straight About Gun Violence and Mental Illness: Putting Compassion Before Fear," *Annals of Internal Medicine*, vol. 159, no. 6, September 17, 2013. |
| Jeff Jacoby | "Crime Soared with Mass. Gun Law," *Boston Globe*, February 17, 2013. |
| Lauren Kirchner | "The Very Weak and Complicated Links Between Mental Illness and Gun Violence," *Pacific Standard*, January 23, 2015. |
| David Kopel | "Guns, Mental Illness and Newton: There Were 18 Random Mass Shootings in the 1980s, 54 in the 1990s, and 87 in the 2000s," *Wall Street Journal*, December 18, 2012. |
| Philip Terzian | "In the Presence of Violent Psychotics," *Weekly Standard*, December 18, 2012. |
| Zach Weissmueller | "The Truth About Mental Illness and Guns," Reason.com, November 18, 2013. |
| Fareed Zakaria | "The Solution to Gun Violence Is Clear," *Washington Post*, December 20, 2012. |

OPPOSING
VIEWPOINTS®
SERIES

# CHAPTER 3

# Do Gun Ownership Regulations Reduce Gun Violence?

# Chapter Preface

Restrictions on individual gun ownership in the United States have existed since 1934, when the National Firearms Act (NFA) was passed during the presidency of Franklin D. Roosevelt, in response to the gun violence during Prohibition and the attempted assassination of the president in 1933. The NFA imposed a tax on the transfer of firearms and required registration of certain firearms with the secretary of the treasury. The firearms regulated by the NFA included shotguns and rifles with barrels under eighteen inches in length, machine guns, and firearm mufflers and silencers. The tax and registration were meant to act as deterrents to the acquisition of these firearms, which were seen as highly dangerous and frequently used in crimes.

The Gun Control Act of 1968 (GCA) was passed in response to the high-profile assassinations of President John F. Kennedy in 1963, Martin Luther King Jr. in 1968, and Senator Robert F. Kennedy in 1968. The GCA mandated the federal licensing of companies who sell firearms, except for private individuals selling to another private individual in the same state. The GCA also created a prohibition on selling guns to certain criminals who have served time, fugitives, unlawful drug users, those who have been committed to a mental institution, illegal immigrants, those discharged from the US Armed Forces dishonorably, those who have renounced US citizenship, people with restraining orders against them, and those convicted of misdemeanors and domestic violence.

The Brady Handgun Violence Prevention Act of 1993 created a national background check system to ensure federally licensed dealers were not selling firearms to prohibited persons. The National Instant Criminal Background Check System (NICS) was launched in 1998 and is maintained by the Federal Bureau of Investigation (FBI). Normally the background checks through NICS are completed over the phone or through the Internet instantly, but in cases where there is no definitive clearance, a buyer may have to wait up to three business days.

Despite the aforementioned regulations, the Bureau of Justice Statistics performed a poll of prison inmates in 2004 and found that among prison inmates who used, carried, or possessed a firearm when they committed their crime, only 11 percent obtained their firearm from such legal channels as retail stores, pawn shops, flea markets, and gun shows. Forty percent of the inmates reported that they obtained the gun illegally from a theft, off the street, or from the black market. Almost the same amount—37 percent—said they obtained the gun from a family member or friend.

A 2014 poll by Gallup found that 55 percent of Americans were dissatisfied with the nation's laws and policies on guns. Yet, those polled differed in what they thought should be done. Thirty-one percent wanted stricter gun laws, 16 percent wanted less strict gun laws, and 40 percent were satisfied with the current laws. However, with over a quarter million firearms in circulation in the United States, there is a good deal of skepticism about the ability of regulations to keep firearms out of the hands of those who are determined to get them. The authors in the following chapter debate the effectiveness of regulations in reducing gun violence.

*"It is becoming abundantly obvious that merely expanding background checks is not enough. We must strengthen the system itself."*

# Background Checks Need to Be Expanded and Strengthened

## Josh Horwitz

*In the following viewpoint, Josh Horwitz argues that strong background checks are the central component of gun ownership regulations that reduce gun violence. Horwitz claims that there are many indicators of an individual's elevated risk of violence, including past behavior, serious mental illness, and substance abuse. Based on this research, Horwitz says there are several ways to expand and strengthen the existing background check system to keep guns away from dangerous individuals. Horwitz is executive director of the Coalition to Stop Gun Violence and coauthor of* Guns, Democracy, and the Insurrectionist Idea.

As you read, consider the following questions:

1. According to Horwitz, what action was recently taken to close the so-called outpatient commitment loophole?

Josh Horwitz, "Expanding Background Checks Necessary, but Not Enough," *Huffington Post*, March 9, 2014. Copyright © 2014 Coalition to Stop Gun Violence. All rights reserved. Reproduced by permission.

2. How many Americans are shot dead each day in gun homicides, suicides, and accidents, according to the viewpoint?

3. According to the author, when a domestic violence abuser has a firearm, by what factor is the risk of partner homicide increased?

Gun violence prevention efforts got off to a great start in 2014 when the [Barack] Obama administration announced two new executive actions on January 3 that will help keep firearms out of the hands of people at an elevated risk of being a danger to themselves and/or others.

## The Importance of Strengthening Checks

The first executive action helps to clarify that the federal firearm prohibition based on the statutory term "committed to a mental institution," which has always been interpreted to include involuntary inpatient commitments, will now also include involuntary outpatient commitments. The outpatient commitment loophole first came to the nation's attention in 2007, when Virginia Tech [Virginia Polytechnic Institute and State University] gunman Seung Hui-Cho walked through it to legally buy the handguns used in that massacre despite having been committed by a court to an outpatient facility.

The second action clarifies that nothing in the Health Insurance Portability and Accountability Act (HIPAA) would prevent states from notifying the FBI's [Federal Bureau of Investigation's] National Instant Criminal Background Check System (NICS) when a person becomes prohibited from purchasing a firearm based on a court-ordered commitment or other federally disqualifying adjudication. Privacy concerns have been cited repeatedly by the states as a reason they do not forward these adjudications, despite the fact that they contain no actual mental health information. This action will help ensure that the database is more complete moving forward.

Much of the debate since the Newtown [Connecticut] tragedy has focused on *expanding* background checks to cover private transactions of firearms, such as those that occur at gun shows or over the Internet. This is a worthy and necessary goal. Universal background checks are the lynchpin of any successful system designed to prohibit dangerous individuals from accessing firearms.

However, the administration touched on an equally important goal with its recent actions: *strengthening* background checks. In the wake of a series of gruesome mass shootings perpetrated by individuals who *legally* purchased their murder weapons, it is becoming abundantly obvious that merely expanding background checks is not enough. We must strengthen the system itself so that individuals with a history of dangerous behavior can no longer clear its low bar.

## Mass Shooters with Red Flags

One such individual was Aaron Alexis, who legally purchased a shotgun in Virginia and on September 16, 2013, fatally shot 12 people while injuring 3 others at the Navy Yard in Washington, D.C. Alexis had a documented history of mental illness and recklessness with firearms, which included arrests in the states of Texas and Washington. And he's not alone. How many other mass shooters have we now seen legally purchase firearms despite numerous red flags in their background? Seung-Hui Cho, Steven Kazmierczak, Jared Loughner, James Holmes, Wade Michael Page . . . the list goes on and on.

Then there is the daily toll of gun violence we rarely hear about—more than 80 Americans shot dead on a daily basis in gun homicides, suicides and accidents. How many of these lives could be saved if we thoroughly and adequately screen gun buyers for evidence of dangerousness?

If federal and state laws continue to define individuals like George Zimmerman and Aaron Alexis as "good guys with

## A New White House Directive

The president directed federal agencies to make all relevant records, including criminal history records and information related to persons prohibited from having guns for mental health reasons, available to the federal background check system. This effort is beginning to bear fruit. In the first nine months after the president's directive, federal agencies have made available to the NICS [National Instant Criminal Background Check System] over 1.2 million additional records identifying persons prohibited from possessing firearms, nearly a 23% increase from the number of records federal agencies had made available by the end of January [2013].

*White House, "Fact Sheet: Strengthening the Federal Background Check System to Keep Guns Out of Potentially Dangerous Hands," January 3, 2014.*

guns," we know exactly what type of result we are going to get. More bloodshed. More families and communities destroyed by gun violence.

## Signs of an Elevated Risk of Violence

Thankfully, it doesn't have to be this way. Decades of research have identified various behaviors that indicate an elevated risk of violence. Federal law already prohibits some of these individuals from owning and purchasing firearms: convicted felons, fugitives from justice, those under a permanent restraining order, individuals who have been involuntarily committed to psychiatric care, etc. But there are other issues that give rise to an elevated risk of violence that we continue to ignore. Consider the evidence:

- Past violent behavior is a strong predictor of future violence regardless of a diagnosis of mental illness. Individuals convicted of crimes of violence—*including misdemeanors*—are at increased risk of committing future violent crimes.

- Some individuals with serious mental illness, especially those with substance or alcohol abuse disorders and those who have been involuntarily committed for treatment, pose a heightened risk to others when they are experiencing acute exacerbations of their illness.

- Alcohol abuse and illegal use of controlled substances increase the risk of violence toward self and others.

- Most victims of intimate partner homicide are killed with a gun, and evidence has shown that there is as much as a fivefold increased risk of intimate partner homicide when an abuser has a firearm. Yet not all domestic violence restraining orders are prohibitory.

Lawmakers at the federal and state level should be taking advantage of this data to improve the existing background check system. My organization, the Educational Fund to Stop Gun Violence, recently worked with the Consortium for Risk-Based Firearm Policy—a group of mental health and public health experts—to develop a series of recommendations for federal and state legislators based on this evidence.

## The Recommendations

As the consortium points out, legislative initiatives should *not* scapegoat Americans dealing with mental health issues, the overwhelming majority of whom will never become violent in their lifetimes. By focusing on people with elevated risk across the spectrum *instead* of a diagnosis of mental illness, we can strike a balance between a commitment to public safety and respect for the privacy of persons dealing with serious mental illness.

Specifically what should we do to prevent those at elevated risk of violence from purchasing and possessing firearms? Here are the recommendations from the consortium:

- The federal government should clarify that any court-ordered involuntary commitment, including outpatient commitment, should be prohibitory. *Thanks to the Obama administration, this item can now be checked off.*

- State laws should be strengthened to temporarily prohibit individuals from purchasing or possessing firearms after a short-term involuntary hospitalization.

- The process for restoring firearm rights should be modified to better protect the public while being fair to individuals who seek to regain their rights.

- Congress and state legislatures should enact new restrictions on purchase and possession of firearms by individuals found guilty by a court of having engaged in specific criminal offenses shown to be significant risk factors for future violence and by individuals subject to any domestic violence restraining order.

- The current civil restraining order process should be expanded to allow law enforcement and family members to petition a court to authorize seizure of firearms and issue a temporary prohibition on the purchase and possession of firearms based on a specific, substantiated threat of physical harm to self or others.

As Fareed Zakaria recently wrote, "the greatest tragedy" when it comes to gun violence in the United States is that "we know how to [prevent] it," but fail to act. Let us all resolve to make 2014 the year we finally do it.

> "Expanded background checks might well be reasonable, but only if the current system is fixed."

# The "40 Percent" Myth

## John Lott

*In the following viewpoint, John Lott argues that it is a myth that a large number of people who acquire guns in the United States do so without a background check. Lott claims that this figure being circulated by the White House and the media is outdated and relies on faulty research. Lott claims that strengthened checks at the current time will only cause law-abiding citizens who need protection to be unable to get a gun. Lott is a former chief economist at the United States Sentencing Commission and the author of* More Guns, Less Crime: Understanding Crime and Gun Control Laws.

As you read, consider the following questions:

1. According to Lott, what is the faulty fact being circulated by the White House about background checks?

2. Lott claims that the actual percentage of guns purchased in 1993 without going through federally licensed firearm dealers is what?

John Lott, "The '40 Percent' Myth," *National Review Online*, January 24, 2013. Copyright © 2013 National Review Online. All rights reserved. Reproduced by permission.

3. According to the author, what percentage of background checks for gun purchases are not accomplished within two hours?

Gun control advocates have recently been throwing around an impressive new number. President Obama used it last Wednesday, claiming: "as many as 40 percent of guns are purchased without a background check." Vice President Biden and everyone from the *New York Times* to the *Wall Street Journal* to *USA Today* repeatedly use it. That "fact" provided the principal support for his first announced gun control proposal, "universal background checks." But unless you include family inheritances and gifts as "purchases," it is simply false.

The Brady Act background checks currently prevent someone who buys from a federally licensed dealer from buying a gun if he has a felony, or in many cases a misdemeanor conviction, or has been involuntarily committed for mental illness. Prior to Brady, federal law merely required that people sign a statement stating that they did not have a criminal record or a history of mental problems under threat of perjury. Obama's 40 percent claim makes it look like a lot of gun buyers are avoiding these checks.

Actually, the number reported was a bit lower, 36 percent, and as we will see the true number of guns "sold" without check is closer to 10 percent. More important, the number comes from a 251-person survey on gun sales two decades ago, early in the Clinton administration. More than three-quarters of the survey covered sales before the Brady Act instituted mandatory federal background checks on February 28, 1994. In addition, guns are not sold in the same way today that they were sold two decades ago.

The number of federally licensed firearms dealers (FFLs) today is only a fraction of what it was. Today there are only 118,000; while back in 1993 there were over 283,000. Smaller dealers, many operating out of their homes, were forced out by various means, including much higher costs for licenses.

The survey asked buyers if they *thought* they were buying from a licensed firearms dealer. While all FFLs do background checks, those perceived as being FFLs were the only ones counted. Yet, there is much evidence that survey respondents who went to the very smallest FFLs, especially the "kitchen table" types, had no inkling that the dealer was actually "licensed." Many buyers seemed to think that only "brick and mortar" stores were licensed dealers, and thus reported not buying from an FFL when in fact they did.

But the high figure comes primarily from including such transactions as inheritances or gifts from family members. Putting aside these various biases, if you look at guns that were bought, traded, borrowed, rented, issued as a requirement of the job, or won through raffles, 85 percent went through FFLs; just 15 percent were transferred without a background check.

If you include these transfers either through FFLs or from family members, the remaining transfers fall to 11.5 percent.

We don't know the precise number today, but it is hard to believe that it is above single digits.

Nevertheless, even if few purchases avoid background checks, should we further expand the checks? It really depends on how the system would be implemented.

We have to realize that the current system of background checks suffers from many flaws, some causing dangerous delays for people who suddenly need a gun for self-defense, such as a woman being stalked by an ex. In addition to crashes in the computers doing the checks, 8 percent of background checks are not accomplished within two hours, with almost all of these delays taking three days or longer.

Obama made many other false statements during his talk. He asserted that "over the last 14 years [background checks] kept 1.5 million of the wrong people from getting their hands on a gun." But these were only "initial denials," not people prevented from buying guns.

In 2010, the Bureau of Alcohol, Tobacco, and Firearms dropped over 94 percent of those "initial denials" after just preliminary reviews. Virtually all the remaining cases were dropped after further investigation by ATF field offices or the Department of Justice. Few of these "initial denials," 62 people or about 0.1 percent, involved strong enough evidence to be considered for prosecution. Just 13 pleaded guilty or were convicted.

Delays are undoubtedly just an inconvenience for most people buying guns. But for a few, it makes a huge difference in their ability to defend themselves against assailants. Indeed, my own research suggests these delays might actually contribute to a slight net increase in violent crime, particularly rapes.

Clearly, criminals are seldom stopped by the checks. That isn't really too surprising because even when guns were banned in Washington, D.C., and Chicago, or even in island nations such as the U.K., Ireland, and Jamaica, criminals still got guns and murder rates rose after the bans.

No amount of background checks on private transfers would have stopped the Connecticut, Wisconsin, and Colorado massacres.

Expanded background checks might well be reasonable, but only if the current system is fixed. Passing laws may make people feel better, but they can actually prevent people from defending themselves.

| "Guns do much more than kill (in the wrong hands). More often than not, they save lives and prevent violence."

# Allowing Armed Citizens Reduces Gun Violence

*Wayne Allyn Root*

*In the following viewpoint, Wayne Allyn Root argues that Americans use guns to protect themselves many times each year. He claims that armed citizens prevent violence, burglary, and rape. Root contends that felons confirm the deterrent effect of citizens being armed. He claims that although reasonable gun control is acceptable, citizens must be able to arm themselves, and guns should never be banned. Root is a political commentator, radio personality, and author of* The Murder of the Middle Class: How to Save Yourself and Your Family from the Criminal Conspiracy of the Century, *among other titles.*

As you read, consider the following questions:

1. Root cites a 2000 study finding that Americans use guns to defend themselves from crime and violence how many times a year?

Wayne Allyn Root, "Guns Save Lives," *Townhall*, December 23, 2012. Copyright © 2012 Wayne Allyn Root. All rights reserved. Reproduced by permission.

2. The author claims that a survey of felons found that what fraction made the decision not to commit a crime because they feared a potential victim was armed?

3. What gun ban does Root cite to support his view that gun bans are dangerous for citizens?

Why do liberal politicians and the biased liberal mainstream media (meaning pretty much all media in America but FNC [Fox News Channel]) always come to the wrong conclusion, and usually come up with the wrong solution, in response to every crisis? As an example, we don't have a "fiscal cliff" crisis because of a tax problem in America. What we have is a spending problem—[President Barack] Obama is the biggest spender of any politician in world history.

The same story holds true with the gun control issue spurred by the tragic Newtown [Connecticut] school shooting. The liberal politicians and media are using [Chicago mayor] Rahm Emanuel's famous saying, "Never let a crisis go to waste." They are trying to turn a terrible tragedy into a gun problem. Their solution is to try to demonize and ban guns. But the Newtown tragedy wasn't a gun problem, it was a mental illness problem.

Thank goodness the American public has more common sense than the politicians and media big shots. The latest Rasmussen poll is out following the Newtown tragedy. While 27% think stricter gun control laws are the solution, and 15% want limits on violent movies and video games, a dominant 48% believe the answer is more action to treat mental health issues.

## How Americans Defend Themselves

It is obvious that many Americans feel in their gut what the statistics I'm about to share with you *prove*—that guns do much more than kill (in the wrong hands). More often than not, they save lives and prevent violence.

Here are a few proven facts that are too often missing from the gun debate (Thanks to Gun Owners of America and ZeroHedge.com for these statistics):

Based on a 2000 study, Americans use guns to *defend* themselves from crime and violence 989,883 times annually. Banning guns would leave about 1,000,000 Americans defenseless from criminals who have no problem acquiring guns illegally.

A nationwide survey of almost 5000 households found that over a five-year period, 3.5% of households had a member who used a gun to protect themselves, their family, or their property. This also adds up to about the same 1,000,000 incidents annually.

The [Bill] Clinton Justice Department identified 1.5 million cases per year of citizens using guns to defend themselves.

Another survey found that Americans use guns to frighten intruders away from a home break-in about 500,000 times annually.

Armed citizens shoot criminals more than twice as often as police each year (1527 to 606).

Each year about 200,000 women use a gun to defend themselves from a sexual crime or abuse.

The [Jimmy] Carter Justice Department found that of more than 32,000 attempted rapes, 32% were actually committed. But when a woman was armed with a gun or knife, only 3% of the attempted rapes were actually successful.

## How Felons Feel About Guns

Now that we've polled the citizens, how about we see what the felons have to say:

A survey of male felons in 11 state prisons across the USA found that 34% had been scared off, wounded or captured by an armed victim of their crime.

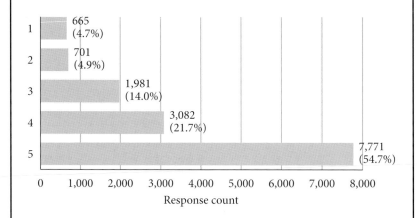

## Law Enforcement's Opinion on Armed Citizens

*On a scale of one to five—one being low and five being high—how important do you think legally armed citizens are to reducing crime rates overall?*

| | |
|---|---|
| 1 | 665 (4.7%) |
| 2 | 701 (4.9%) |
| 3 | 1,981 (14.0%) |
| 4 | 3,082 (21.7%) |
| 5 | 7,771 (54.7%) |

Response count (0, 1,000, 2,000, 3,000, 4,000, 5,000, 6,000, 7,000, 8,000)

TAKEN FROM: PoliceOne, "Gun Policy and Law Enforcement Survey," March 4–13, 2013.

40% of felons made a decision not to commit a crime because they feared the potential victim had a gun.

69% of felons knew other fellow criminals who had been scared off or captured by an armed victim.

57% of felons polled agreed that "criminals are more worried about meeting an armed victim than they are about running into the police."

Statistical comparisons with other countries show that burglars in the United States are far less apt to enter an occupied home than their foreign counterparts who live in countries where fewer civilians own firearms.

These facts (and many more too voluminous to show here) prove that guns—in the right hands—defend citizens, families, and children. In short, *guns save lives.*

## The Danger of Gun Bans

But for me, it's always been a personal and emotional argument, even more than a factual one. I'm a proud Jewish American. Over six million of my fellow Jews were enslaved, starved, tortured, and then slaughtered by Adolf Hitler. Before it could happen, in 1938, Hitler banned gun ownership for Jews.

That act on November 11, 1938, (one day after the infamous Kristallnacht) was the beginning of the end for Germany's Jews. Millions of Jews were left defenseless from that day forward. Just like the criminals in the studies above, who were far less likely to break into a home or attack a victim if they feared the victim was armed, Hitler only started his murderous genocide after first ensuring his victims were disarmed, defenseless, and helpless.

Will a conservative NRA (National Rifle Association [of America]) and JPFO (Jews for the Preservation of Firearms Ownership) member like me support reasonable gun control? *Of course.* Should we ensure that mentally ill people cannot purchase guns? *Of course.* Should we enforce current gun laws? *Of course.* Should we do more to ensure that all gun owners are licensed, trained, responsible and mentally competent? *Of course.* Should we take lessons from Israel's gun laws that require strict mental evaluation and examinations, as well as rigorous training? *Absolutely.*

But should we move to ban guns, thereby leaving the law-abiding citizens defenseless and helpless? Never. Not in America.

Should government and law enforcement be the only ones legally able to carry guns? Never. Not in America.

Should government be allowed to take away guns from honest, law-abiding homeowners, business owners, and citizens like me? Only when you pry them from my cold, dead hands.

Thomas Jefferson put it best: "When governments fear the people, there is liberty. When the people fear the government, there is tyranny."

> *"Attempts by armed civilians to stop shooting rampages are rare—and successful ones even rarer."*

# Allowing Armed Citizens Does Not Reduce Gun Violence

*Mark Follman*

*In the following viewpoint, Mark Follman argues that evidence does not support the view that armed civilians can stop mass shootings. In fact, Follman claims, the rise in gun ownership and loosening of gun regulations in recent years correlate with an increase in shootings. Follman maintains that armed civilians are likely to do more damage than good in a shooting and that it would be better to focus on treating mass shootings like a public health emergency, enacting measures to increase public safety. Follman is a senior editor at* Mother Jones.

As you read, consider the following questions:

1. According to Follman, how many mass shootings over the last thirty years did *Mother Jones* investigate?

2. What percentage of states now recognize handgun permits from at least some other states, according to the author?

Mark Follman, "More Guns, More Mass Shootings—Coincidence?," *Mother Jones*, December 15, 2012. Copyright © 2012 Mother Jones. All rights reserved. Reproduced by permission.

3. Of the mass shootings analyzed, according to the author, approximately what fraction of the shooters killed themselves?

In the fierce debate that always follows the latest mass shooting, it's an argument you hear frequently from gun rights promoters: If only more people were armed, there would be a better chance of stopping these terrible events. This has plausibility problems—what are the odds that, say, a moviegoer with a pack of Twizzlers in one pocket and a Glock in the other would be mentally prepared, properly positioned, and skilled enough to take out a body-armored assailant in a smoke- and panic-filled theater? But whether you believe that would happen is ultimately a matter of theory and speculation. Instead, let's look at some facts gathered in a five-month investigation by *Mother Jones*.

## Armed Citizens and Mass Shootings

In the wake of the massacres this year [2012] at a Colorado movie theater, a Sikh temple in Wisconsin, and Sandy Hook Elementary School in Connecticut, we set out to track mass shootings in the United States over the last 30 years. We identified and analyzed 62 of them, and one striking pattern in the data is this: In not a single case was the killing stopped by a civilian using a gun. And in other recent (but less lethal) rampages in which armed civilians attempted to intervene, those civilians not only failed to stop the shooter but also were gravely wounded or killed. Moreover, we found that the rate of mass shootings has increased in recent years—at a time when America has been flooded with millions of additional firearms and a barrage of new laws has made it easier than ever to carry them in public places, including bars, parks, and schools.

America has long been heavily armed relative to other societies, and our arsenal keeps growing. A precise count isn't possible because most guns in the United States aren't registered and the government has scant ability to track them, thanks to a legislative landscape shaped by powerful pro-gun groups such as the National Rifle Association [of America (NRA)]. But through a combination of national surveys and manufacturing and sales data, we know that the increase in firearms has far outpaced population growth. In 1995 there were an estimated 200 million guns in private hands. Today, there are around 300 million—about a 50 percent jump. The US population, now over 314 million, grew by about 20 percent in that period. At this rate, there will be a gun for every man, woman, and child before the decade ends.

There is no evidence indicating that arming Americans further will help prevent mass shootings or reduce the carnage, says Dr. Stephen Hargarten, a leading expert on emergency medicine and gun violence at the Medical College of Wisconsin. To the contrary, there appears to be a relationship between the proliferation of firearms and a rise in mass shootings: By our count, there have been two per year on average since 1982. Yet, 25 of the 62 cases we examined have occurred since 2006. In 2012 alone there have been seven mass shootings, and a record number of casualties, with more than 140 people injured and killed.

Armed civilians attempting to intervene are actually more likely to increase the bloodshed, says Hargarten, "given that civilian shooters are less likely to hit their targets than police in these circumstances." A chaotic scene in August at the Empire State Building put this starkly into perspective when New York City police officers trained in counterterrorism confronted a gunman and wounded nine innocent bystanders in the process.

## A Loosening of Gun Restrictions

Surveys suggest America's guns may be concentrated in fewer hands today: Approximately 40 percent of households had them in the past decade, versus about 50 percent in the 1980s. But far more relevant is a recent barrage of laws that have rolled back gun restrictions throughout the country. In the past four years, across 37 states, the NRA and its political allies have pushed through 99 laws making guns easier to own, carry, and conceal from the government.

Among the more striking measures: Eight states now allow firearms in bars. Law-abiding Missourians can carry a gun while intoxicated and even fire it if "acting in self-defense." In Kansas, permit holders can carry concealed weapons inside K–12 schools, and Louisiana allows them in houses of worship. Virginia not only repealed a law requiring handgun vendors to submit sales records, but the state also ordered the destruction of all such previous records. More than two-thirds of these laws were passed by Republican-controlled statehouses, though often with bipartisan support.

The laws have caused dramatic changes, including in the two states hit with the recent carnage. Colorado passed its concealed-carry measure in 2003, issuing 9,522 permits that year; by the end of last year the state had handed out a total of just under 120,000, according to data we obtained from the County Sheriffs of Colorado. In March of this year, the Colorado Supreme Court ruled that concealed weapons are legal on the state's college campuses. (It is now the fifth state explicitly allowing them.) If former neuroscience student James Holmes were still attending the University of Colorado today, the movie theater killer—who had no criminal history and obtained his weapons legally—could've gotten a permit to tote his pair of .40-caliber Glocks straight into the student union. Wisconsin's concealed-carry law went into effect just nine months before the Sikh temple shooting in suburban Milwaukee this August. During that time, the state issued a whopping 122,506 permits, according to data from Wisconsin's Department of Justice. The new law authorizes guns on college campuses, as well as in bars, state parks, and some government buildings.

## The Reciprocity of State Laws

And we're on our way to a situation where the most lax state permitting rules—say, Virginia's, where an online course now qualifies for firearms safety training and has drawn a flood of out-of-state applicants—are in effect national law. Eighty percent of states now recognize handgun permits from at least some other states. And gun rights activists are pushing hard for a federal reciprocity bill—passed in the House late last year, with GOP vice-presidential candidate Paul Ryan among its most ardent supporters—that would essentially make any state's permits valid nationwide.

Indeed, the country's vast arsenal of handguns—at least 118 million of them as of 2010—is increasingly mobile, with 69 of the 99 new state laws making them easier to carry. A decade ago, seven states and the District of Columbia still prohibited concealed handguns; today, it's down to just Illinois and DC. (And Illinois recently passed an exception cracking the door open to carrying.) In the 62 mass shootings we analyzed, 54 of the killers had handguns—including in all 15 of the mass shootings since the surge of pro-gun laws began in 2009.

In a certain sense, the law was on their side: Nearly 80 percent of the killers in our investigation obtained their weapons legally.

## The Reality of Mass Murders

We used a conservative set of criteria to build a comprehensive rundown of high-profile attacks in public places—at schools, workplaces, government buildings, shopping malls—though they represent only a small fraction of the nation's overall gun violence. The FBI [Federal Bureau of Investigation] defines a mass murderer as someone who kills four or more people in a single incident, usually in one location (as opposed to spree or serial killers, who strike multiple times.) We excluded cases involving armed robberies or gang vio-

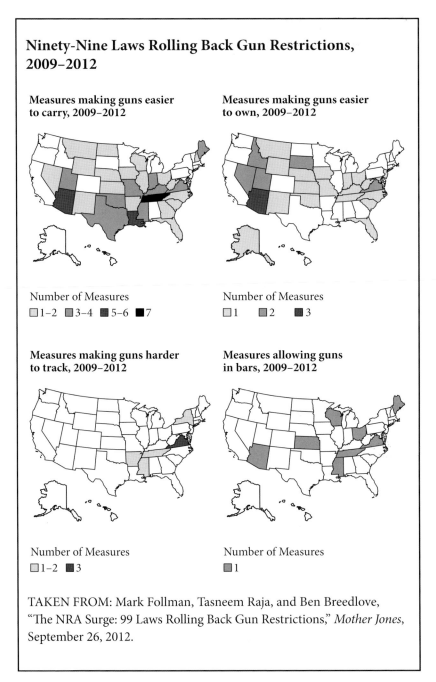

### Ninety-Nine Laws Rolling Back Gun Restrictions, 2009–2012

**Measures making guns easier to carry, 2009–2012**

Number of Measures
☐ 1–2  ☐ 3–4  ■ 5–6  ■ 7

**Measures making guns easier to own, 2009–2012**

Number of Measures
☐ 1  ☐ 2  ■ 3

**Measures making guns harder to track, 2009–2012**

Number of Measures
☐ 1–2  ■ 3

**Measures allowing guns in bars, 2009–2012**

Number of Measures
☐ 1

TAKEN FROM: Mark Follman, Tasneem Raja, and Ben Breedlove, "The NRA Surge: 99 Laws Rolling Back Gun Restrictions," *Mother Jones*, September 26, 2012.

lence; dropping the number of fatalities by just one, or including those motives, would add many, many, more cases.

There was one case in our data set in which an armed civilian played a role. Back in 1982, a man opened fire at a welding shop in Miami, killing eight and wounding three others before fleeing on a bicycle. A civilian who worked nearby pursued the assailant in a car, shooting and killing him a few blocks away (in addition to ramming him with the car). Florida authorities, led by then state attorney Janet Reno, concluded that the vigilante had used force justifiably, and speculated that he may have prevented additional killings. But even if we were to count that case as a successful armed intervention by a civilian, it would account for just 1.6 percent of the mass shootings in the last 30 years.

More broadly, attempts by armed civilians to stop shooting rampages are rare—and successful ones even rarer. There were two school shootings in the late 1990s, in Mississippi and Pennsylvania, in which bystanders with guns ultimately subdued the teen perpetrators, but in both cases it was after the shooting had subsided. Other cases led to tragic results. In 2005, as a rampage unfolded inside a shopping mall in Tacoma, Washington, a civilian named Brendan McKown confronted the assailant with a licensed handgun he was carrying. The assailant pumped several bullets into McKown and wounded six people before eventually surrendering to police after a hostage standoff. (A comatose McKown eventually recovered after weeks in the hospital.) In Tyler, Texas, that same year, a civilian named Mark Wilson fired his licensed handgun at a man on a rampage at the county courthouse. Wilson— who was a firearms instructor—was shot dead by the body-armored assailant, who wielded an AK-47. (None of these cases were included in our mass shootings data set because fewer than four victims died in each.)

## The Opinion of Law Enforcement

Appeals to heroism on this subject abound. So does misleading information. Gun rights diehards frequently credit the end of a rampage in 2002 at the Appalachian School of Law in Virginia to armed "students" who intervened—while failing to disclose that those students were also current and former law enforcement officers, and that the killer, according to police investigators, was out of bullets by the time they got to him. It's one of several cases commonly cited as examples of ordinary folks with guns stopping massacres that do not stand up to scrutiny.

How do law enforcement authorities view armed civilians getting involved? One week after the slaughter at the *Dark Knight Rises* screening [at a movie theater in Aurora, Colorado] in July [2012], the city of Houston—hardly a hotbed of gun control—released a new Department of Homeland Security–funded video instructing the public on how to react to such events. The six-minute production foremost advises running away or otherwise hiding, and suggests fighting back only as a last resort. It makes no mention of civilians using firearms.

Law enforcement officials are the first to say that civilians should not be allowed to obtain particularly lethal weaponry, such as the AR-15 assault rifle and ultrahigh-capacity, drum-style magazine used by Holmes to mow down Batman fans. The expiration of the Federal Assault Weapons Ban [formally known as the Public Safety and Recreational Firearms Use Protection Act] under President George W. Bush in 2004 has not helped that cause: Seven killers since then have wielded assault weapons in mass shootings.

## A Public Health Emergency

But while access to weapons is a crucial consideration for stemming the violence, stricter gun laws are no silver bullet. Another key factor is mental illness. A major *New York Times* investigation in 2000 examined 100 shooting rampages and found that at least half of the killers showed signs of serious mental health problems. Our own data reveals that the majority of mass shootings are murder-suicides: In the 62 cases we analyzed, 36 of the shooters killed themselves. Others may have committed "suicide by cop"—seven died in police shootouts. Still others simply waited, as Holmes did in the movie theater parking lot, to be apprehended by authorities.

Mental illness among the killers is no surprise, ranging from paranoid schizophrenia to suicidal depression. But while some states have improved their sharing of mental health records with federal authorities, millions of records reportedly are still missing from the FBI's database for criminal background checks.

Hargarten of the Medical College of Wisconsin argues that mass shootings need to be scrutinized as a public health emergency so that policy makers can better focus on controlling the epidemic of violence. It would be no different than if there were an outbreak of Ebola virus, he says—we'd be assembling the nation's foremost experts to stop it.

But real progress will require transcending hardened politics. For decades, gun rights promoters have framed measures aimed at public safety—background checks, waiting periods for purchases, tracking of firearms—as dire attacks on constitutional freedom. They've wielded the gun issue so successfully as a political weapon that Democrats hardly dare to touch it, while Republicans have gone to new extremes in their party platform to enshrine gun rights. Political leaders have failed to advance the discussion "in a credible, thoughtful, evidence-driven way," says Hargarten.

In the meantime, the gun violence in malls and schools and religious venues continues apace. As a superintendent told his community in suburban Cleveland this February, after a shooter at Chardon High School snuffed out the lives of three students and injured three others, "We're not just any old place, Chardon. This is every place. As you've seen in the past, this can happen anywhere."

> *"Without conducting a background check, private sellers have no way of knowing if they are selling to a prohibited purchaser."*

# The Private Gun Sale Loophole Needs to Be Closed

*Mayors Against Illegal Guns*

*In the following viewpoint, Mayors Against Illegal Guns argues that the current background check system for firearm purchases has a loophole that allows any individual to purchase a gun online from private sellers without a background check. The author contends that this loophole is allowing thousands of guns to be sold to potential felons, domestic abusers, and others who should be prohibited from purchasing firearms. Mayors Against Illegal Guns, a program of Everytown for Gun Safety, is made up of hundreds of current and former mayors united in their belief that more should be done to keep guns out of the hands of dangerous people.*

"Felon Seeks Firearm, No Strings Attached," Mayors Against Illegal Guns, September 2013, pp. 8–13. Copyright © Everytown for Gun Safety Support Fund 2013. All rights reserved. Reproduced by permission.

As you read, consider the following questions:

1. The author cites the National Survey on Private Owner-ship and Use of Firearms, which found that what per-centage of recent gun buyers did not have a background check?

2. The investigation of online would-be buyers performed by Mayors Against Illegal Guns found that what fraction had committed crimes that prohibited them from pos-sessing a gun?

3. The author estimates that the online site Armslist hosts approximately how many unique firearm ads in a year?

Under federal law, several classes of particularly dangerous individuals are prohibited from firearm possession—including felons, the seriously mentally ill, domestic abusers and drug addicts. The names of prohibited purchasers are contained in NICS [National Instant Criminal Background Check System], a system of databases operated by the Federal Bureau of Investigation [FBI], and licensed gun dealers are re-quired to run the names of would-be buyers through NICS before they complete their sales.

## A Two-Tiered System

This system is efficient and effective. Despite the gun lobby's claims that checks impose a burden on buyers, filling out the paperwork and completing a background check takes just a few minutes. During an attempted purchase, the dealer phones the NICS call center or submits the buyer's information to NICS through its web-based E-Check system. Phone calls to NICS are answered within seven seconds, on average, and more than 90 percent are resolved immediately while the dealer is on the phone. If a buyer's name is in NICS because he is federally prohibited, NICS will instruct the dealer to deny the sale, without revealing any other information about the would-be buyer.

Since its creation in 1998, NICS has blocked more than two million gun sales to criminals and other prohibited purchasers.

But not all gun sellers are required to conduct background checks. Under federal law, licensed firearms dealers must do so, but unlicensed sellers who are not "in the business" of selling firearms are exempt.

This two-tiered system has created a vast secondary market, leaving a large share of firearms sales completely unregulated. National telephone surveys and law enforcement data suggest that some 40 percent of gun transfers do not involve a licensed dealer—meaning an estimated 6.6 million guns were transferred without background checks in 2012. The National Survey on Private Ownership and Use of Firearms, a telephone survey of 2,568 individuals funded by the Department of Justice, showed that 37 percent of recent gun buyers had obtained their gun in a transfer that did not require a check. Similarly, according to Michigan State Police, 48 percent of state handgun transfers are conducted without a licensed dealer. This amounts to more than 50,000 private-party handgun transfers each year in Michigan alone.

## The Online Market for Guns

The unregulated private market for guns is flourishing in a range of commercial settings, including gun shows—temporary exhibitions where firearms and accessories are bought and sold in person—and websites, where a buyer needs little more than a phone number or email address to buy a gun.

Online sales are a vast and growing share of the firearms market. More than a decade ago, the Justice Department estimated that guns were sold online at 80 firearm auction sites and about 4,000 other websites. The number of active sites has grown immeasurably in the years since.

A simple web search will return hundreds of online storefronts operated by individual licensed dealers; online brokers like eBay that mediate sales between buyers and sellers; and classified aggregators where would-be buyers and sellers post ads, such as Armslist, the 'Craigslist' for guns. While there is no authoritative estimate of the total number of firearms sold online each year, the number of gun ads listed by private sellers on Armslist has expanded almost sevenfold within the last twenty months—from 12,000 in December 2011 to 83,000 active ads in August 2013.

In most respects, online gun sales are subject to the same rules as other gun sales. If a prospective buyer wants to buy a gun online from a licensed dealer, the buyer must pass a background check—typically conducted in person at a local dealership—before taking possession of the gun. Transferring a gun between people from different states also usually involves a background check because federal law prohibits private sellers from shipping guns across state lines directly to would-be buyers. In such cases, the seller typically ships the gun to a licensed dealership in the buyer's state, where the dealer runs a check on the buyer before giving them the gun.

But federal law does not require private sellers to conduct background checks when they sell to in-state buyers: They can meet face-to-face and exchange guns for cash with no questions asked. And websites like Armslist—where the vast majority of the listings are posted by private sellers—are designed to help buyers find private sellers in their home states.

## Illegal Online Sales by Private Sellers

Without conducting a background check, private sellers have no way of knowing if they are selling to a prohibited purchaser. A first-of-its-kind investigation by New York City in 2011 shed light on how online private sales play out in practice. The investigation found that a majority of private online sellers have no qualms about selling guns to people who admitted they were prohibited purchasers.

The city's investigators called 125 private sellers in 14 states advertising guns on 10 websites, including Armslist. During each conversation, the investigators told the sellers that they probably could not pass a background check. Fully 62 percent of these sellers agreed to sell the gun anyway, though it is a felony to sell a firearm to a person the seller has reason to believe is a prohibited purchaser. Fifty-four percent of the private sellers who posted ads on Armslist were willing to sell guns to people who admitted they were prohibited purchasers.

In the wake of the 2011 investigation and the subsequent mass shooting at Sandy Hook Elementary School in Newtown, Connecticut, one of the websites the city examined—KSL, managed by Deseret Media Companies—suspended firearms listings on its classified ads pages. Craigslist, which had officially barred firearm sales but still featured thousands of gun ads at the time of the investigation, also appears to have strengthened its system for flagging and removing firearms listings.

While the 2011 investigation demonstrated that online private sales provide ample opportunity for prohibited purchasers to buy guns, there has been no measure of how many criminals are exploiting this loophole. This investigation provides the first snapshot of the problem.

## The 'Want-to-Buy' Ads

Despite the size and significance of the private firearms market, little public data is available about private online gun sales, including the extent to which prohibited purchasers use websites to avoid background checks.

The vast majority of ads on sites like Armslist are posted by sellers, but would-be buyers can also post ads that describe the guns they seek (known as 'want-to-buy' or WTB ads). These ads offer a window on would-be buyers in the private online gun market.

To learn more about would-be gun buyers online, this investigation reviewed a *unique data set: the identifying information voluntarily provided by would-be gun buyers in want-to-buy ads on Armslist.*

## An Investigation of the Ads

Armslist is a large, national online marketplace where private sellers and buyers exchange guns. The website hosts tens of thousands of gun ads from every state, and nearly all of them are posted by private sellers. In want-to-buy ads, the prospective buyer typically describes a firearm he is seeking and sellers make contact through the website; some want-to-buy ads also provide a phone number or email address.

Our investigators 'scraped' (a software technique for extracting online data) 13,298 want-to-buy ads for firearms posted on Armslist from February 11, 2013, to May 10, 2013, and examined them for identifying information. Unique phone numbers or email addresses were found in 1,430 of the ads. Using reverse lookup phone data, 607 of those identifiers could be linked to an individual living in the state where the ad was placed.

Investigators then conducted criminal record checks on each individual by searching court records in the geographic areas where the individual was known to have maintained a current or past address. Any felony convictions, domestic violence misdemeanor convictions, bench warrants or orders of protection that could be linked to the individual were subjected to legal analysis to determine if they prohibited possession of firearms under federal law.

To ensure that matches between would-be gun buyers and criminal records were valid, investigators called the phone number posted in each ad to confirm that the subscriber had placed the ad, and that their name and date of birth matched the criminal record. This step eliminated six individuals who had placed ads but were incorrectly linked to prohibiting criminal records—for example, because they listed a phone number that belonged to someone else, or because a former phone subscriber had a criminal record but the person who posted the ad did not.

## The Actual Scope of the Problem

Due to unavoidable limitations of this methodology, the investigation's results considerably understate the actual scope of the problem.

*Conservative sample.* Criminal gun buyers seeking to remain anonymous are more likely to browse for-sale ads and contact sellers directly rather than posting their own ads and divulging their contact information. As a result, the share of want-to-buy ads placed by criminals almost certainly underestimates the total share of online gun buyers that are prohibited from purchasing guns.

*Limited scope of records reviewed.* Investigators only examined criminal records in the jurisdictions where the subscriber was known to have maintained a residence, so individuals who committed prohibiting crimes in other jurisdictions were not identified. Nor did the investigators examine records of noncriminal prohibiting criteria, including serious mental illness, drug abuse, dishonorable discharge from the armed forces and immigration status.

*Mismatched records.* Criminal gun buyers may have posted ads online but listed the phone number of a friend or family member with a clean record. In such cases, they would not have been identified as prohibited, resulting in an undercount of criminal buyers. Investigators did not make follow-up calls to apparently non-prohibited buyers to ensure that they were, in fact, the person who placed the ad.

## The Results of the Investigation

*Of 607 would-be gun buyers, 3.3 percent—1 in 30—had committed crimes that prohibited them from possessing a firearm. To put this number in context, if 1 in 30 people on a Boeing 747 were on a terrorist watch list, the plane would have 22 suspected terrorists aboard.*

Looking at other scenarios in which government assigns risks and takes steps to ameliorate them is also insightful. Regulators and private industry routinely intercede when consumer products present hazards to health or safety that are far smaller than those posed by the online private sale loophole.

In 2010, Toyota recalled more than two million vehicles after receiving complaints of unintended acceleration at a rate of 72 per 100,000 vehicles sold—a 1 in 1,389 risk of failure. In January 2013, Fisher-Price voluntarily recalled 800,000 Newborn Rock 'n Play Sleepers because of concerns about mold after receiving 600 complaints—1 in 1,333 at risk. And in November 2010, the Food and Drug Administration recalled the drug propoxyphene because it appeared to increase the risk of drug-related deaths over a five-year period by 6 per 100,000 compared to an alternative medication—a 1 in 16,667 increase in absolute risk.

The 1-in-30 chance of selling a gun to a criminal on Armslist is an order of magnitude greater than these.

## Examples of Prohibited Buyers

Many of the prohibited buyers identified in the investigation had lengthy criminal histories that included recent violent crimes:

- A 25-year-old male in Louisiana posted an ad on March 21, 2013, offering to "meet face to face" and promising "cash in hand." A review of his criminal record revealed that a month earlier, he had been charged with aggravated assault with a firearm, a felony. Two days prior to posting the ad, he had been charged with illegally carrying a weapon, also a felony. A month after posting the ad, he received a third charge, for domestic

## The Danger of the Private Sale Loophole

In October 2012, Zina Daniel obtained a restraining order against her husband, Radcliffe Haughton, who had a history of abusing her. The restraining order prohibited him from buying a gun under federal law.

But several days later, he placed a 'want-to-buy' ad on Armslist, met a private seller, and bought a Glock .40-caliber semiautomatic handgun without a background check.

The following day, Zina was at her job in a spa in a Brookfield, Wisconsin, mall when Haughton burst in, shooting and murdering her and two other women and injuring four others before killing himself.

*Mayors Against Illegal Guns,*
*"Felon Seeks Firearm, No Strings Attached,"*
*September 2013.*

abuse battery. Each of these offenses was sufficient to disqualify him from possessing firearms.

- A 25-year-old male in Columbus, Ohio, posted an ad on March 24, 2013, offering "cash, ammo, or a combo of both for payment." Criminal records indicate that he was named as a defendant in 15 felony or misdemeanor cases between 2007 and 2013, including pending charges for aggravated robbery and drug possession and repeated charges of illegal gun possession. He also pled guilty to possession of crack cocaine in 2010, a felony that prohibited him from buying guns.

- A 27-year-old male in Fort Collins, Colorado, posted an ad on March 30, 2013, seeking an M&P22 handgun. In

2005, the would-be buyer had attacked his ex-girlfriend and was found guilty of domestic violence harassment; he later violated an order of protection. Both offenses barred him from purchasing or possessing firearms.

- A 35-year-old male in North Carolina posted an ad for an M1A SOCOM 16 rifle on March 27, 2013, insisting on meeting "face to face ONLY." The would-be buyer had been arrested as a fugitive in Iowa in 2003 and extradited to North Carolina; he was also found guilty of a series of felony charges, including robbery with a dangerous weapon, in 1996. These offenses rendered him a prohibited purchaser.

- A 27-year-old in Louisville, Kentucky, posted an ad on March 28, 2013, in search of an XD(M) 3.8″ handgun, promising "will pay cash." In 2006, he had been found guilty in Ohio of misdemeanor assault against the mother of his child, which prohibited him from possessing firearms. He had also been convicted twice for drug abuse.

## Comparing Online Sales to Sales by Licensed Dealers

The estimated share of criminals seeking guns in private, online sales is dramatically higher than those who try to buy from licensed gun dealers. In 2012, licensed dealers conducted 8,725,425 federal background checks. 76,260 of these potential sales—0.87 percent—were blocked because the check revealed a history of crime or domestic violence. By contrast the share of buyers seeking guns on Armslist who are prohibited for those reasons is *nearly four times higher*.

One likely explanation for this disparity is that the background check system is successfully deterring criminals from attempting to buy from licensed dealers and driving them to private online sales. Indeed, sites like Armslist make it easy to avoid background checks by allowing users to limit searches to ads listed by private parties with the click of a button.

This explanation is consistent with another development: The share of background checks conducted by licensed dealers that result in denial has been declining since the system became operational in 1998, even though the NICS database has become more comprehensive. It is possible that this decline reflects a migration of prohibited purchasers away from licensed dealers—and background checks—and toward unregulated private sellers.

Laws that require background checks for private sales close off this avenue to criminals. And indeed, states that have passed their own laws requiring background checks for private sellers have lower rates of gun violence and crime than states that have not.

Critics of the background check system sometimes suggest that if the system were expanded to cover private sales, some persistent criminals would simply take their search to the black market. This may be true. But research shows that, contrary to conventional wisdom, buying guns on the black market is neither cheap nor easy. Criminals report paying $250 to $400 on the black market for guns valued at only $50 to $100 in the legal market; the quality of these firearms is less reliable; and conducting these transactions poses substantial risk of harm or arrest. A study of underground gun markets in Chicago found that more than one in three attempts to buy a gun from a black market dealer ended in failure.

## The Arming of Criminals

On an average day, more than 2,000 new gun ads are posted on Armslist. At the present rate, Armslist alone will host 790,000 unique firearm ads in 2013.

This investigation of would-be gun buyers who post ads and voluntarily include identifying information suggests that a minimum of 1 in 30 gun buyers on the website have committed crimes which prohibit them from purchasing guns.

*At this prevalence, gun sales transacted on a single website may put at least 25,000 guns into the hands of criminals—and likely many more—this year alone.*

## Recommendations to Close the Loophole

Congress must act to close the loophole that allows criminals to buy guns online without a background check. And the Bureau of Alcohol, Tobacco, Firearms and Explosives (ATF) and the websites that host these gun marketplaces must do their part, too.

- *Congress should enact legislation to require a background check for every commercial gun sale, including those facilitated by websites.* The existing background check system is efficient and effective, but limited: As long as private sales remain exempt from this commonsense requirement, criminals will exploit this loophole and wreak havoc on American communities. Bipartisan legislation under consideration by both chambers of Congress—sponsored in the Senate by Joe Manchin (D-WV) and Pat Toomey (R-PA) and in the House by Representatives Peter King (R-NY) and Mike Thompson (D-CA)—would enact the necessary reform.

- *ATF should improve enforcement of existing laws.* This investigation shows that criminals are arming themselves online every day. ATF should use all the tools at its disposal to interdict illegal online sales, including by conducting undercover investigations of websites that sell guns, documenting when guns recovered from crimes were originally sold online and offering online tutorials to train sellers and buyers about the laws governing online sales.

- *Websites should adopt tougher protocols to deter crime.* The Internet has created enormous opportunities for businesses and vastly expanded the choices available to individual consumers. But online actors should meet the same public safety standards they are required to satisfy in the brick-and-mortar marketplace. Websites that host gun ads can do so by demanding transparency from their sellers and buyers, flagging suspicious behavior, and taking reasonable steps to ensure they are not facilitating illegal gun sales to criminals. Strategies some websites already employ include requiring visitors to register before viewing or posting ads; asking buyers and sellers to complete a verification process to confirm their identity; and providing features that allow users to easily flag suspicious activity for review by site administrators.

I *"What they call a 'loophole' is really your right to privacy."*

# Treating Personal Transfers Like Retail Sales Would Violate Rights

*Dave Kopel*

*In the following viewpoint, Dave Kopel argues that the attempts to get background checks on all gun transfers in the nation, including those between private parties, is really an attempt to have nationwide gun registration in order to make future confiscation easier. Kopel contends that this attempt at further government involvement threatens individual rights to gun ownership and to privacy. Kopel is research director of the Independence Institute, an associate policy analyst with the Cato Institute, and an adjunct professor at the University of Denver's Sturm College of Law.*

As you read, consider the following questions:

1. According to Kopel, to sell firearms across state lines, federal law mandates what?

Dave Kopel, "Ever Wonder What a Loophole Looks Like?," *America's 1st Freedom*, June 2012. Copyright © 2012 Dave Kopel. All rights reserved. Reproduced by permission.

2. What three countries does Kopel cite as examples of places where gun registration records have been used for gun bans?

3. What evidence does the author give to support his claim that those in favor of gun control want not only background checks but also gun owner registration?

Should the government keep lists of people who exercise their constitutional rights? If you write a letter to a newspaper, or join a church, or possess a firearm, should your name be entered into a government database?

## The Push to Close the Private Sale "Loophole"

According to the gun prohibition lobbies, every gun and every gun owner must be registered by the government. They accurately recognize that confiscation of some or all firearms is very difficult without comprehensive gun registration. To get comprehensive registration, they must close the "loophole" that allows private transfers of firearms.

Legislation introduced in the U.S. Senate by Charles Schumer, D-N.Y., and vigorously promoted by [New York City mayor] Michael Bloomberg's gun-ban group "Mayors Against Illegal Guns" would help accomplish the prohibitionists' objectives. The House version of the bill, H.R. 1781, has 86 co-sponsors, nearly a fifth of all U.S. representatives.

And don't count on the Supreme Court to stop any of this. [The 2008 case upholding individual gun rights, *District of Columbia v.*] *Heller* is one vote away from being overturned, and if President Barack Obama is reelected, the odds of him being able to appoint a replacement for one of the five pro–Second Amendment justices are pretty strong. Justice Antonin Scalia is 76 years old, and Justice Anthony Kennedy is 75.

Make no mistake, the gun prohibition groups aim to close the "loophole" that prevents the government from creating lists of all guns and those who own them.

The existence of the so-called "loophole" starts with the fact that the federal government does not impose upon ordinary people the special laws that apply to federally licensed firearm dealers.

## Federal Gun Control Laws

Let's start with some basics. Most federal gun control laws are based on the power that the Constitution gives Congress "[t]o regulate Commerce . . . among the States." Pursuant to this power, Congress enacted a statute (the Gun Control Act of 1968) that says private individuals may not sell (or otherwise transfer) firearms across state lines. In order to sell a firearm across state lines, at least one party to the transaction must have a federal firearms license (FFL). ("FFL" is the standard abbreviation for both the license itself and for the licensee.)

So an FFL is, by definition, a licensed person engaged in the interstate commerce of firearms. It is only an FFL, for example, who can buy guns from a wholesaler or manufacturer and then retail them to the general public.

Federal law imposes various requirements on FFLs. They must keep records of every sale they make, and these records are subject to inspection by the federal Bureau of Alcohol, Tobacco, Firearms and Explosives (BATFE). Before completing a sale, the FFL must contact the FBI's [Federal Bureau of Investigation's] National Instant Criminal Background Check System (NICS), or its state equivalent, and obtain authorization.

If you are "engaged in the business" of selling firearms, then you *must* have an FFL. Otherwise, every single sale would be a serious federal felony. Federal law defines "engaged in the business" as repeated transactions for profit. In contrast, a person is not engaged in the business of dealing in firearms if he or she makes "occasional sales, exchanges or purchases of firearms for the enhancement of a personal collection or for a hobby, or who sells all or part of his personal collection of firearms. . . ." 18 U.S.C. §921(a)(21)(C). And if you aren't "engaged in the business," you can't get an FFL.

## The Law for Private Sellers

So for regular people who occasionally sell guns (e.g., a person who sells one of his rifles to a friend in a hunting club), the special laws for firearm businesses do not apply. The seller does not need to keep a record of the sale, the seller is not subject to warrantless inspection by the BATFE and the seller does not need to get prior permission from the government for the sale. At the same time, the occasional seller does not enjoy the privilege, which FFLs have, of being able to buy or sell guns across state lines.

It's just common sense that the special laws that apply to businesses with a federal license do not apply to ordinary people who are not in the business and therefore cannot obtain the federal license.

Regardless of whether you have an FFL or not, one federal law does always apply: It is a felony to transfer a gun to someone if you have "reasonable cause" to believe that the individual is a "prohibited person." A prohibited person is someone who is prohibited by federal law from possessing a gun; examples include convicted felons, illegal aliens, persons who have been adjudicated mentally defective and so on.

The large majority of states have similar laws that distinguish between professional firearm dealers and persons who occasionally sell or give away a personal firearm.

## The Use of Gun Registration Records

The gun prohibition lobbies are not happy with this situation. One of the problems, from their point of view, is that when an individual sells a gun to his cousin or neighbor, there is no mandatory record keeping for the transaction. This means that there is no registration of the gun. And without registration, confiscation is much more difficult.

Pete Shields, who was then head of the group that now calls itself the Brady Campaign [to Prevent Gun Violence], explained in 1976: "The first problem is to slow down the number of handguns being produced and sold in this country. The second problem is to get handguns registered. The final problem is to make possession of all handguns and all handgun ammunition—except for the military, police, licensed security guards, licensed sporting clubs and licensed gun collectors—totally illegal" (Richard Harris, "A Reporter at Large: Handguns," *New Yorker*, July 26, 1976, p. 58).

The existence of private sales is not the only impediment to gun registration. Thanks to the NRA [National Rifle Association of America], several federal laws forbid the compilation of a federal gun registry—whether from the sales records kept by FFLs or through [NICS]. However, the gun prohibition lobbies can always hope that the federal anti-registration laws will be repealed. Besides that, they can hope that the federal government will just start compiling instant check records to form at least a partial federal registry, as the [Bill] Clinton administration tried to do.

Besides that, the gun prohibition lobbies have convinced a minority of states to collect data from licensed firearm dealers in order to create state gun registries. Usually, these involve only handguns. Two states—California and Rhode Island—have gone all the way, so that every firearm transfer, even between private individuals, will lead to the creation of a permanent government record.

There's no doubt that gun registration records do get used for gun bans. That has been the experience not only in Canada and Europe, but also in the United States. For example, since 1966, all firearms in New York City have had to be registered. In 1991, then mayor David Dinkins rammed his version of an "assault weapons" ban through the city council. The 1966 registration law was used by the police to enforce the 1991 prohibition.

More recently, in June 1999, newspapers found documents from extremist antigun California attorney general Bill Lockyer showing the intent to use registration lists to confiscate so-called "assault weapons," which had been registered according to the request of the previous attorney general. After the documents were leaked, Lockyer's office promptly denied they were drafted for any purpose other than "for discussion."

## The "Gun Show Loophole"

For more than a decade, the gun prohibition lobbies have been concentrating, with success in some states, on the so-called "gun show loophole." The prohibitionists, such as Mayor Michael Bloomberg, claim that gun shows are some sort of weekend Brigadoon, in which none of the normal gun laws apply and sales take place without any controls.

This is just the opposite of the truth. The laws about selling guns at gun shows are exactly the same as everywhere else. If you are "engaged in the business," then all the rules about sales that would apply at your business premises also apply when you sell at a gun show. Conversely, if you are a widow who is selling her husband's collection, then you are not engaged in the business and you can rent a table at a gun show without being subject to all the special rules that apply to business owners.

The attack on the "gun show loophole" is just the opening round in an attack on all private sales. The leadership of Colorado's affiliate of the national gun ban groups was caught on tape explaining that the group's gun show initiative was an "incremental" step toward the goal of requiring government approval for all firearm transfers, even those between two private individuals.

Moreover, the antigun groups use the "gun show loop-hole" issue to perform their standard bait-and-switch. According to the Colorado law that was successfully pushed by the gun ban groups, any time there are three people present, that's a "gun show." Thus, a "gun show" can be a gathering in Aunt Mary's home for the purpose of distributing her recently deceased husband's collection of firearms, even if the only people present are Aunt Mary, a nephew and a niece.

So the words "gun show loophole" are really a disguise for gun control laws that have nothing to do with gun shows. So, too, is the "private sales loophole."

## The Proposed Act

For example, Bloomberg's flagship bill in Congress is the mis-named "Fix Gun Checks Act," introduced by Schumer. Here are some of the things that the Bloomberg/Schumer bill, S. 436, would do in the supposed name of requiring background checks for private gun sales:

It would be a federal felony to temporarily allow someone to use or hold your firearm in the following circumstances:

- *While a friend visits your home*

- *While taking a friend target shooting on your property, or on public lands where target shooting is allowed*

- *While instructing students in a firearm safety class*

The bill would also ban gun possession by anyone who has ever been ordered to receive counseling for any mental problem.

This would include:

- *A college student who was ordered to get counseling because the school administration was retaliating against him for criticizing the administration*

- *An adult who was ordered to receive counseling in fifth grade for stuttering, attention deficit disorder or mathematics disorder*

- *A woman who was raped in an elevator, and now has a phobia about elevators*

Also in the name of "fixing" gun checks, Bloomberg and Schumer would overturn the constitutional standards of due process and fair trial. Their bill would prohibit gun ownership based on any drug arrest rather than on convictions. Thus, S. 436 would make gun possession a felony for a person who was once arrested for marijuana possession and was later found innocent because a police officer mistook tobacco for marijuana.

## The Right to Privacy

The antigun groups sometimes claim that they are only asking for background checks on private transfers. But when they actually get that, they don't want it, unless the background checks can be used for registration. For example, in June 1999, the U.S. House of Representatives was considering a comprehensive gun control bill. An amendment was added that imposed background checks on private sales at gun shows—but which forbade the FBI to keep registration records of law-abiding gun owners. The gun prohibition groups and their congressional allies were outraged, so they helped kill the bill.

It's also interesting to note that should all private sales ever become subject to government approval through the background check system currently in place for FFLs, *all* legal gun sales in the nation could immediately be halted by the government simply shutting down the background check system, whether intentionally or by accident, for only a few hours or a much longer period of time. That's an ominous scenario, indeed.

The gun ban groups have learned a lot about persuasive language over the years. These days, they rarely use the phrase "gun control," since "control" is not a popular term among the liberty-minded American public. Instead, the groups target uninformed people, including some gun owners, by describing various aspects of firearm freedom as "loopholes."

But what they call a "loophole" is really your right to privacy—a right that helps protect your lawful firearms from the gun confiscation lobby.

# Periodical and Internet Sources Bibliography

*The following articles have been selected to supplement the diverse views presented in this chapter.*

| | |
|---|---|
| C.J. Ciaramella | "Concealed Carry on Campus: Nowhere Is Perfectly Safe—Give the Kids a Fighting Chance," *Weekly Standard*, May 5, 2010. |
| Charles C.W. Cooke | "Norway and Gun Control: Gun Laws Do Not Hit Their Target," *National Review Online*, July 27, 2011. |
| Brian Doherty | "Gun Control Couldn't Have Stopped It," *Reason*, April 2011. |
| Sean Faircloth | "Why More Guns Won't Make Us Safer," *The Week*, February 2, 2013. |
| Mark Hemingway | "Is It True Armed Civilians Have Never Stopped a Mass Shooting?," *Weekly Standard*, December 20, 2012. |
| Robert A. Levy | "A Libertarian Case for Expanding Gun Background Checks," *New York Times*, April 26, 2013. |
| John R. Lott Jr. | "Brady Law Has Done Little to Keep Guns Out of Criminals' Hands," *Investor's Business Daily*, March 3, 2014. |
| Gary C. Sackett | "Common Sense Weapons Bill That Would Make Us Safer," *Salt Lake Tribune*, May 27, 2011. |
| William Saletan | "Friendly Firearms," *Slate*, January 11, 2011. |
| Doug Thompson | "Another Gun Law Would Not Have Saved Those in Tucson," *Capitol Hill Blue*, January 12, 2011. |

OPPOSING
VIEWPOINTS®
SERIES

# CHAPTER 4

# What Should Be Done to Reduce Gun Violence?

# Chapter Preface

Any regulations undertaken to reduce gun violence must be in accordance with the US Constitution. The Second Amendment of the Constitution was adopted in 1791. It reads: "A well-regulated Militia, being necessary to the security of a free State, the right of the people to keep and bear Arms, shall not be infringed." Since its adoption, there has been debate about whether the right identified by the Second Amendment refers to an individual right to own guns or a collective right of the people to have arms for use in the military. Legally, the US Supreme Court has settled the issue in recent years, and any regulations on guns in the United States cannot outright ban gun ownership. Nonetheless, certain restrictions are constitutional.

The landmark 2008 case *District of Columbia v. Heller* solidified the understanding of the right identified in the Second Amendment as protecting "an individual right to use arms for self-defense." The court distinctly noted that states and municipalities may not ban handguns: "Handguns are the most popular weapon chosen by Americans for self-defense in the home, and a complete prohibition of their use is invalid." The court noted, however, that there may be certain restrictions on gun ownership: "Like most rights, the right secured by the Second Amendment is not unlimited," and "nothing in our opinion should be taken to cast doubt on long-standing prohibitions on the possession of firearms by felons and the mentally ill, or laws forbidding the carrying of firearms in sensitive places such as schools and government buildings, or laws imposing conditions and qualifications on the commercial sale of arms."

Although the court's decision may have calmed the debate about banning guns, it has not brought any clarity to the debate about gun control. Just what regulations ought to limit gun ownership remains a controversy. Many of the current gun ownership restrictions were created by legislation established years ago: The Gun Control Act of 1968 created a prohibition on selling guns to certain criminals, unlawful drug users, mentally ill individuals, and illegal immigrants. The Brady Handgun Violence Prevention Act of 1993 created a national background check system to help prevent firearm sales to such prohibited persons. As the authors of the viewpoints in the following chapter illustrate, the current debate about how to reduce gun violence is fraught with controversy, with no clear consensus on how to proceed.

> *"Gun violence in America is a national plague that we urgently need to eradicate."*

# Gun Regulations Are Necessary and Allowed Under the Second Amendment

## Mark Nuckols

*In the following viewpoint, Mark Nuckols argues that although the United States seems to take sharp notice of gun violence when a mass shooting occurs, there is reason to be concerned about gun violence that occurs every day. Nuckols contends that the gun lobby has convinced the public and politicians that the Second Amendment supports near unrestricted gun ownership, but he argues that this interpretation of the amendment is not true and more regulations are needed. Nuckols is a professor of law and business at the Lomonosov Moscow State University Business School and at the Russian Presidential Academy of National Economy and Public Administration.*

As you read, consider the following questions:

1. On a typical day in the United States, how many people are murdered by guns, according to the author?

Mark Nuckols, "New Gun Laws? Don't Aim at Only Mass Shootings Like Sandy Hook," *Christian Science Monitor*, December 19, 2012. Reprinted with permission of the author.

2. What did the US Supreme Court recently decide regarding the constitutionality of gun regulations, according to Nuckols?

3. What two groups of people does Nuckols single out as potentially posing a risk of harm to themselves or others?

Year after year, nearly 100,000 Americans are shot or killed in gun-related incidents. That is the equivalent of a war—one waged in US communities and homes on a daily basis.

## The Daily Bloodshed

But we only take notice of the grim toll inflicted by widespread and largely unregulated gun ownership when the violence is sufficiently spectacular to attract major media coverage. So when 20 young children and six adults are murdered in a shooting spree in a grade school in a quiet Connecticut community [Newtown], as well as the gunman killing himself and his mother, the entire nation is appalled by such random and massive violence.

However, on a typical day in the United States, 33 people are murdered by guns, and another 50 die in gun-related suicides.

And there are three specific groups of people who are the most common victims of gun violence: the wives and girlfriends of men who own guns, young inner-city African-American men, and people who suffer from clinical depression—though random mass shootings remind us that others, too, are vulnerable.

It is a sad commentary that the spectacular series of shootings in classrooms, malls, and theaters—rather than the more widely destructive everyday incidents—could be the galvanizing force that finally moves America to sensible gun regulation. But regulate America must.

As a nation, the US has failed to do anything meaningful to stop this senseless bloodshed. The public has been hoodwinked by an ideological campaign based on misleading arguments, and politicians have been cowed by the gun lobby. But as New York mayor Michael Bloomberg rightly commented after the Newtown, Conn., tragedy, the power of the National Rifle Association [of America] is "vastly overrated."

## The Arguments of the Gun Lobby

For decades, the gun lobby has loudly proclaimed that the Second Amendment protects an individual right to gun ownership. Only recently has the Supreme Court actually endorsed this interpretation, and the court held only that the federal and local governments cannot impose absolute bans on gun ownership, emphatically emphasizing that the Constitution does not prohibit strict regulation of gun ownership.

Regulation of guns is in fact almost entirely a political issue, for which a wide range of politicians have dodged responsibility by hiding behind a largely fictional cover of constitutionality that supposedly disallowed regulation.

Another common argument is that hunting and sport shooting is a sacred "way of life" for gun owners. But isn't "hobby" a more accurate term?

My own preferred hobby is driving my Volvo 850 at 140 miles per hour. Law-abiding and responsible gun owners protest that their legal enjoyment of guns should not be constrained by restrictive gun legislation. I am a responsible and law-abiding driver and the speed limits on America's highways deprive me of the pleasure of high velocity auto travel, which I can enjoy on the autostrada when I visit Italy but not when I am on US Interstate 95. Yet I respect the right of my fellow citizens to impose a speed limit in the interests of public safety.

One other oft-heard argument in support of unrestricted gun ownership is that gun owners can stand against internal

© Mike Peters Editorial Cartoon used with the permission of Grimmy, Inc. and the Cartoonist Group. All rights reserved.

tyranny or external military threat. The idea that random Americans wielding personal firearms—or even a group or groups of armed Americans—might constitute a viable military force may work for Hollywood, but not in reality.

But even a recent historical example—Slovenia's 1991 fight for independence from Yugoslavia—was entirely based on the mobilization of local Slovenian police and the country's national guard in order to succeed. The better way to guarantee and participate in political liberty or national security in the US is through civic participation or military service.

## The Dangers of Lax Regulations

The need to better restrict access to guns is urgent. Millions of Americans suffer from depression or have serious problems with controlling anger—a vast pool of people who potentially pose a risk of harm to themselves or to others that is needlessly exacerbated by the easy availability of guns.

And tens of thousands of Americans are seriously mentally ill, and categorically should not be allowed to own firearms. Yet we tolerate such seriously ineffective barriers to gun purchasing that even deeply troubled people can walk into a Wal-Mart and buy a Smith & Wesson. Background checks and data entries must be much more thorough.

Violent crime in America has been declining since the early 1990s. Still, it is far greater in the US than in other industrialized countries. This criminal violence is needlessly amplified by a thriving illegal black market in guns that is facilitated by lax regulation of gun sales. In effect, states such as Virginia that permit promiscuous, multiple gun purchases are exporting murder and mayhem into cities like Baltimore, Philadelphia, and New York.

Legislators in such states must now respond to the facts, as reported by a study underwritten by 300 US mayors. The 2008 study found that states with lax gun laws had more sales of weapons used in crimes in other states than did states with more strict regulations (the lax states also had higher rates of handgun killings and of fatal shootings of police officers).

A rational analysis of the immense social costs of unregulated gun ownership shows they far exceed the benefits gun ownership confers. Arguing otherwise is to say a weekend hobby of hunting or target practice is more important than the lives of 20 schoolchildren or tens of thousands of other Americans. Or that profits from selling handguns by the dozen are more important than the rights of millions of inner-city residents to live in relative security.

Gun violence in America is a national plague that we urgently need to eradicate. Let Newtown be the new day for gun regulation, beginning with a return to outlawing assault weapons, the very kind that shooter Adam Lanza used to such devastating effect.

> "Government bears a heavy burden to
> justify any regulations that would com-
> promise our right to bear arms."

# Gun Regulations Are Ineffective and Threaten the Second Amendment

*Robert A. Levy*

*In the following viewpoint, Robert A. Levy argues that the right to bear arms under the Second Amendment is a fundamental right. Levy contends that certain gun control proposals, such as bans on high-capacity magazines and assault weapons, are ineffective and unconstitutional. He claims that most gun ownership regulations do not lower gun violence, and he suggests two policies that would lower gun violence. Levy is chairman of the Cato Institute's board of directors and coauthor of* The Dirty Dozen: How Twelve Supreme Court Cases Radically Expanded Government and Eroded Freedom.

As you read, consider the following questions:

1. According to Levy, what does it mean to say that the right to bear arms is a fundamental right?

Robert A. Levy, "Our Core Second Amendment Rights," *Cato's Letter*, v. 11, no. 3, summer 2013. Copyright © 2013 Cato's Letter. All rights reserved. Reproduced by permission.

2. What kinds of guns does the author say have essentially been banned since 1934?

3. Beyond legalizing drugs, what policy does the author suggest to lessen gun violence?

The Second Amendment to the United States Constitution secures an individual right to bear arms for self-defense. That was the holding in the landmark decision issued by the Supreme Court in *District of Columbia v. Heller.*

Furthermore, that protection now applies everywhere in the United States. At the time of the framing, the Bill of Rights applied only to the federal government. We soon learned, however, that the states can be every bit as tyrannical as the Feds, slavery being the obvious case in point. In a series of cases after the Civil War, the Fourteenth Amendment was used to "incorporate" the Bill of Rights—that is, to make most of its provisions enforceable against the states. For the first time, the federal government could intervene if the states violated our rights.

## A Fundamental Right

Interestingly, it wasn't until *McDonald v. City of Chicago* in 2010 that the Supreme Court decided that the Second Amendment applies everywhere, to the states as well as federal jurisdictions like Washington, D.C.

The right to bear arms, however, is not absolute. Like other provisions of the Bill of Rights, it's subject to reasonable restrictions. Nevertheless, the Supreme Court declared in both *Heller* and *McDonald* that the right to bear arms is considered a "fundamental right." What does that mean? It means individuals enjoy a presumption of liberty. Government bears a heavy burden to justify any regulations that would compromise our right to bear arms. That point was central to a ruling in December 2012 by the U.S. Court of Appeals in *Moore v. Madigan*, which overturned the Illinois ban on concealed-carry of firearms. The state, said the court, failed to meet its burden of proof.

## A Ban on High-Capacity Magazines

With that as a brief background, let's look at some of the current gun control proposals that are pending before both Congress and state legislatures. Take, for instance, high-capacity magazines. It's not difficult to imagine multiple-victim killings—like the ones in Newtown[, Connecticut]—where innocent lives might have been saved if we had an effective ban on high-capacity magazines. The key word, of course, is "effective." An ineffective ban is worse than useless because it deters only law-abiding citizens. So what restrictions should be allowed?

That's where the burden of proof is critical. It is up to the government to compile data indicating whether the benefits of banning high-capacity magazines exceed the costs. If they do, and if the government can produce relevant evidence, I have little doubt that a ban on large magazines would survive a Second Amendment court challenge. But there are three related problems.

First, homemade magazines are very easy to assemble. They are essentially a box with a spring in it. Second, there is no way to confiscate the millions of high-capacity magazines that are currently in circulation. Third, existing semiautomatic handguns are typically configured to use magazines with 11 to 19 rounds. A ban on any size less than 20 would therefore make these weapons dysfunctional and encounter great resistance.

That said, I'm not aware of any situation where an actual or potential civilian victim has fired more than 20 rounds in self-defense. Weapons with more than 20 rounds have been used several times in these random mass killings. Evidence like that might be sufficient for government to justify a 20-

round limit. There is a proposal now in Congress which calls for a 10-round limit, and New York law has such a limit—with the added caveat that you can only have seven of those rounds actually loaded in the magazine. Those laws should both be rejected.

## A Ban on Assault Weapons

What about an assault weapons ban? This is once again a matter of empirical evidence. We had an assault weapons ban from 1994 to 2004. Seven months after it expired, the *New York Times*—no fan of gun rights—reported that "despite dire predictions that the streets would be awash in military-style guns, the expiration of the decade-long assault weapons ban last September has not set off a sustained surge in the weapons' sales . . . [or] caused any noticeable increase in gun crime."

We currently have millions of so-called assault weapons in circulation, used by Americans for everything from hunting and self-defense to target shooting and Olympic competition. Criminals do not typically use assault rifles. They use handguns. Assault weapons are expensive and very difficult to conceal. And even if we were to reinstitute the ban, we would be unable to deal with the huge number of these guns already owned.

Some people argue in favor of a buyback program. As you can imagine, that would be extraordinarily costly. Furthermore, who would the sellers be? They would be people who valued the money more than they valued the firearm, and that would be mostly low-income persons who need the money. These individuals often live in high-crime areas and obey the law, but they need a means to defend themselves. By the same token, who would keep their weapons under a buyback program? They'd be individuals who valued their weapons more than the money, which would include criminals and terrorists for whom guns are a tool of the trade.

In the *Heller* case, Justice [Antonin] Scalia suggested that the Second Amendment would pose no barrier to outlawing weapons that are either especially dangerous or not in common use. So it's quite clear that certain firearms can be banned. Indeed, automatic weapons—those guns that continue to fire after pulling the trigger once—have essentially been banned since 1934. The task, therefore, in structuring an assault weapons ban is to cover only those firearms that are not commonly used, are not needed for self-defense, and would improve public safety if banned. The 1994 assault weapons ban quite clearly went too far, but a much better crafted and more limited version might be justified.

To put this in perspective, however, there were almost 13,000 people murdered with a weapon in 2011. Of those, 1,700 were killed with knives; 500 were killed with hammers, bats, and clubs; and 728 by someone's bare hands. How many of those were killed with rifles—not just assault rifles, but rifles of all types? Three hundred and twenty-three. I don't mean to trivialize 323 deaths, but banning popular semiautomatic rifles merely because they come equipped with a pistol grip or another feature that has no effect on the weapon's lethality makes no sense whatsoever.

## The Extension of Background Checks

What about the clamor to extend background checks to private sales, which includes purchases at gun shows, over the Internet, and through published ads? Survey data indicates that less than 2 percent of guns used by criminals are bought at gun shows and flea markets—a figure that includes sales through licensed gun show dealers, which are already subject to background checks. Yet the *New York Times* still editorializes that background checks "prevented nearly 2 million gun sales over a 15-year period." This is an incredible claim. There is no way for the *Times* to know how many sales were prevented from occurring. Violence-prone buyers who don't pass a background check will purchase elsewhere or steal a gun. Peaceful buyers who don't pass their background check, however, might be unable to defend themselves with an appropriate firearm.

In 2010 the National Instant Criminal Background Check System (NICS) denied 76,000 would-be buyers. How many of those individuals were prosecuted? Forty-four out of 76,000. How many convicted? Thirteen out of 76,000. That is a conviction rate of 0.02 percent, which suggests two possibilities. Either the remaining denials were legitimate purchases that were unjustly blocked by the NICS system or, if the denials were proper, then somehow 99.98 percent of those 76,000 rejected applicants escaped punishment. Most likely both factors were at work. But neither of those possibilities offers much hope for an expanded system of background checks. We would do much better to improve the existing system.

I have two further points regarding background checks. First, if they actually promoted public safety, then taxpayers should foot the bill, not law-abiding gun owners. Second, the claim that background checks just take a few minutes is disingenuous. Many of the checks take up to 72 hours. Most gun shows are two-day events. In some cases, the real goal of the expanded checks was to drive gun shows out of business. That strategy has been partially successful. Yet its advocates know that if they tried to implement a law banning gun shows, it would be deemed unconstitutional.

You have to remember that the "I" in NICS stands for "instant." If technology could facilitate truly rapid background checks—with a 24-hour maximum—I'd have no objection to extending NICS checks to cover selected private sales. But I have no illusions that this would curb violence. Rather, I believe that accepting rapid checks—as proposed in the [Joe] Manchin–[Pat] Toomey compromise bill earlier this year— would have conferred significant benefits on gun rights advocates in return for modest concessions. In short, the compromise bill would have been superior to the legal regime we have now.

## The Enactment of Effective Policies

That said, what policies would actually be effective? The most effective option, which is rarely considered, is to legalize drugs. This would result in a huge reduction in gun violence. There are 1.5 million drug arrests each year, with more drug inmates than all violent criminals combined. Because drugs are illegal, participants in the drug trade cannot go to court to settle their disputes. Those disputes are instead resolved on the streets with guns. The Drug Enforcement [Administration] currently has about 10,000 agents, analysts, and support staff, men and women who could be involved in fighting real crime or terrorism instead.

Another alternative suggested by the National Rifle Association [of America] is arming guards at school. Israel has done that and school violence is effectively zero. Keep in mind that about 28 percent of our public schools already employ security officers who carry guns, so this isn't a new idea. For the remaining schools, retired military and police personnel make for obvious recruits. The focus should be on entrance security, which would involve less manpower. We don't need an armed guard in every classroom.

It's true, of course, that an armed guard didn't prevent Columbine [referring to a mass school shooting at Columbine High School in Colorado in 1999]. But neither did the ban on assault weapons or the ban on high-capacity magazines that were also in effect at that time. In fact, gun-free school zones have been a magnet for the mentally deranged. We have armed guards at banks, airports, power plants, courts, stadiums, government buildings, and of course on planes. There's no reason why we couldn't have armed guards at those schools that decided they need them.

In the aftermath of this heart-wrenching tragedy at Sandy Hook [referring to the mass school shooting at Sandy Hook Elementary School in Newtown, Connecticut], we need to evaluate our gun laws by all means. But I am skeptical about the efficacy of gun regulations, mostly because they are imposed almost exclusively on those who are not part of the problem. We need to remember that our core Second Amendment rights are at risk. We therefore need to be absolutely certain that the ends justify the means.

> "What is needed is an approach that fo-
> cuses tightly on altering the behavior of
> criminals."

# More Law Enforcement, Not More Regulation, Reduces Gun Violence

*Steve Chapman*

*In the following viewpoint, Steve Chapman argues that stricter gun regulation will not solve the problems of mass shootings and street-gun violence. Chapman contends that proposals for banning certain guns would never be tolerated in the United States and are ineffective at stopping violence. He claims that increased law enforcement and certain police programs, however, have been shown to be effective at reducing the presence of guns and gun violence. Chapman is a columnist and editorial writer for the* Chicago Tribune.

As you read, consider the following questions:

1. Chapman contends that the United States will never adopt ultra-stringent gun regulations of the sort seen in what two countries?

Steve Chapman, "The Right Way to Combat Gun Violence," Reason.com, February 25, 2013. Copyright © 2013 Creators Syndicate. All rights reserved. Reproduced by permission.

2. The author explains that the addition of more police officers in New York City reduced homicides by what percentage since 1990?

3. How much cash does Chapman suggest giving tipsters for providing police with information about criminals and illegal guns?

Public policy is a lot like math: No matter what the problem, the wrong answers are far more numerous than the right ones. This is particularly true on the subject of mass shootings and other firearms violence, which have stimulated a new fervor for barking up the wrong tree.

## The Problem with Stricter Gun Regulation

Many liberals think the answer to mass shootings and street crime lies in stricter gun regulation: banning "assault weapons," limiting the capacity of magazines or, in their unrestrained moments, adopting ultra-stringent laws like those in [Great] Britain or Australia.

But most of these ideas are irrelevant or impossible. Even if the Second Amendment didn't prevent it, Americans would never stand for a near-total ban on ownership of semiautomatic weapons, à la Australia, or of handguns, as in Britain. You might as well expect Nebraska to build 300 miles of oceanfront beaches.

Outlawing "military-style" guns would be a waste of time, since other weapons of identical capabilities would remain available. A limit on magazine capacity wouldn't impede street thugs, who don't need to fire 30 rounds to accomplish their tasks, or even mass shooters, who typically bring multiple guns or magazines.

The problem with most gun control laws is that they impose a burden on the law-abiding that lawbreakers can usually evade. What is needed is an approach that focuses tightly on altering the behavior of criminals. There are proven steps that can hobble the dangerous without penalizing the harmless.

## The Importance of Law Enforcement

What works in preventing violent crime? One remedy is simple, though not cheap: more police on the streets. This may look like a Blinding Flash of the Obvious, but it's not. Among criminologists, it was once commonly assumed, based on actual research, that beefing up patrols would make no difference.

Today, the evidence points conspicuously in the opposite direction. Jens Ludwig, who directs the Crime Lab at the University of Chicago, says, "The COPS [Community Oriented Policing Services] program launched in the 1990s under President [Bill] Clinton helped contribute to the crime drop we saw in that decade." Nationally, it increased the number of police by more than 80,000.

New York City added 7,000 uniformed officers in the 1990s, and its numbers are still well above where they started. Result: a stunning 81 percent reduction in homicides since 1990. Last year [2012], the city had fewer murders than any year since 1963. In January, it went 10 days without a single homicide.

Having plenty of law enforcement personnel is just part of the battle; the other part is using them effectively. What appears to have worked in New York—and, later, in Chicago—is swarming crime "hot spots" with cops for days or weeks, forcing criminals to mind their manners. This approach "almost certainly made a substantial contribution in New York," writes criminologist Franklin Zimring, author of *The City That Became Safe*.

It was once thought that when cops moved into an area, crooks would merely move to another one. It turns out that migration is not always an attractive option. So a crime prevented today may be a crime that is never committed.

## The Impacts of Hot Spots Policing

Police . . . emphasized 'hot spots,' a strategy that had proved effective in other cities and that almost certainly made a substantial contribution in New York. Starting in 1994, the city also adopted a management and data-mapping system called CompStat. At a central office in downtown Manhattan, analysts compile data on serious crimes, including their exact locations, and map them to identify significant concentrations of crime. Patrols then deploy in full force on-site—whether it is a sidewalk, a bar or any other public place—sometimes for weeks at a time, systematically stopping and frisking anyone who looks suspicious and staring down everyone else. Although one might expect that criminals would just move to another street and resume their business as usual, that is not what happened in New York.

*Franklin E. Zimring,*
*"How New York City Beat Crime,"*
Scientific American, *August 2011.*

## A Carrot-and-Stick Approach

Chicago also had some luck with a joint federal-city operation, called Project Safe Neighborhoods [PSN]. It zeroed in on ex-convicts, with the goal of dissuading them from carrying guns, using a carrot-and-stick approach. The stick was federal prosecution carrying long sentences with no parole in faraway prisons; the carrot was meetings where offenders were offered help getting shelter, job training, and education.

In areas where PSN was implemented, homicide rates plunged. In the rest of the city, they barely budged. Ex-offenders who were required to take part in roundtable meetings with police, community representatives and service providers were nearly 30 percent less likely than others to end up back in prison.

Another method of catching thugs with guns, says Ludwig, is to offer significant cash rewards to tipsters—$500 or $1,000. This approach would not only produce more arrests of felons and teens but also strongly discourage them from illegally carrying weapons. An action that today may generate respect or fear—displaying a handgun to friends or rivals—would suddenly carry a serious risk of prison time.

If we hope to reduce gun crime, the answer doesn't lie in broad laws that mostly affect people who pose no threat. It lies in targeting the criminals. Most gun control measures involve rearranging the haystack. What these initiatives do is locate the needles.

> "If not a ban on assault weapons now, then when?"

# Shame on U.S.: How Many Tiny Coffins Do We Need Next Time?

*Mike Lupica*

*In the following viewpoint, Mike Lupica argues that the killing of twenty-six people—primarily young children—in Newtown, Connecticut, in December 2012, brought to clear light the need to ban assault weapons like the kind used by the killer. Lupica claims that the strength of the National Rifle Association of America (NRA) has created cowardly politicians who will not enact a sensible ban on assault weapons. He marvels at the failure to pass legislation banning these weapons in the aftermath of the Newton tragedy. Lupica is a sports columnist for the* New York Daily News.

As you read, consider the following questions:

1. What kind of gun did the 2012 Newtown school shooter use, according to Lupica?

Mike Lupica, "Shame on U.S.: How Many Tiny Coffins Do We Need Next Time?," *New York Daily News*, March 20, 2013, p. 4. Copyright © 2013 Daily News, L.P. (New York). All rights reserved. Reproduced by permission.

2. Approximately how many lives does Lupica estimate might have been saved in Newtown if the killer did not have an assault weapon?

3. What politician does the author identify as a longtime proponent of gun control who compromised on the assault weapons ban?

This is what an emotional President Obama said in a gym in Newtown, Conn., on a Sunday night in December, two days after 26 people—20 of them children—were murdered in cold blood by Adam Lanza, all of the killing done by a semi-automatic rifle called the AR-15:

"We can't tolerate this anymore. We are not doing enough and we will have to change."

Then he looked out into the audience and into the faces of the families of the victims of Sandy Hook Elementary School and said this to them, and to the country:

"I'll use whatever power this office holds . . . in an effort aimed at preventing more tragedies like this."

But what does the president say now to the families of the victims of Sandy Hook, and Aurora, Colo., and all the other victims of mass murders and glory killers in this country? What does he say now that it becomes clear that a ban on assault weapons won't even be legitimately included in the gun legislation being shaped this week in the U.S. Senate?

Any fool knows that Lanza couldn't possibly have killed as many children as quickly as he did on the morning of Dec. 14 without an assault weapon in his hands. So how does the president and any other big politician who allows the gun nuts from the National Rifle Association to win again answer the larger question about weapons that make killings like the elementary-school massacre ridiculously easy:

If not now for a ban for these weapons, when?

If Sandy Hook Elementary doesn't make every member of Congress take a stand against assault weapons in this country, then what does? How many small coffins do we need the next time?

And after the next Adam Lanza shows up with a gun like an AR-15 in a school or a theater or a shopping mall, no one will believe a word the president says at the next memorial service about profoundly changing gun laws in this country. Because three months after Newtown, it turns out that the president has no real power to change anything when it comes to guns in the hands of the wrong people in America.

Of course background checks are important. But so is an assault weapons ban. And please don't believe the self-serving and slobbering supporters of the NRA—that means all the politicians in the House and the Senate who have pimped themselves out to the NRA—who tell you that a ban like this won't make a difference, will not save lives the next time.

That happens to be a shameful and gutless lie.

Again: Ask any gun owner if Lanza could have killed as many children as he did in as short a time as he did—before he was a sure shot putting a bullet from one of his handguns through his snake-filled brain—if he didn't have an AR-15 in his hands. Then go ask the gun lovers to explain all over again how a ban on weapons like this wouldn't have saved three young lives that morning, or five, or maybe even more than that.

We know how much money the NRA pours into lobbying for guns like this to be completely available in America. We know that it has turned so many politicians, too many politicians, into cowards in the face of the money and imagined power of the NRA. But what dollar value would the NRA put on the life of a single child who could have been saved that morning if Adam Lanza had only been firing away with a handgun?

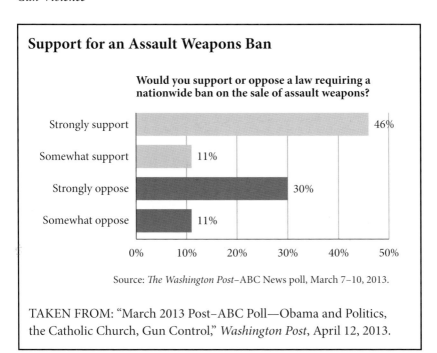

**Support for an Assault Weapons Ban**

**Would you support or oppose a law requiring a nationwide ban on the sale of assault weapons?**

| | |
|---|---|
| Strongly support | 46% |
| Somewhat support | 11% |
| Strongly oppose | 30% |
| Somewhat oppose | 11% |

Source: *The Washington Post*–ABC News poll, March 7–10, 2013.

TAKEN FROM: "March 2013 Post–ABC Poll—Obama and Politics, the Catholic Church, Gun Control," *Washington Post*, April 12, 2013.

All we get now on guns in Washington is pathetic deal making. We see even tough, noble politicians fighting for the ban, such as Sen. Dianne Feinstein (D-Calif.), giving up on the assault weapons ban because it is too controversial, and will perhaps kill the chance for other gun restrictions that do have bipartisan support.

Feinstein has fought for more gun control for such a long time and was nearly in tears Tuesday when talking about the failure of the ban to even make it to the Senate floor as anything more than an amendment in a much bigger gun bill.

"People say, 'well, are you disappointed?'" Feinstein said. "Obviously, I'm disappointed."

Wayne LaPierre of the NRA, the face and voice opposing gun control in America, yammers on constantly about how only good guys with guns can stop bad guys with guns, as if the only way to make us all safer from killing machines like Lanza are more guns. But you have to know this was a day in Washington when the bad guys won, and won big.

There is a reason why nearly 140,000 print and online readers of the *Daily News* signed petitions in this newspaper's campaign to ban assault weapons and high-capacity magazines. It is because they believed—and properly so—that this moment, the moment of Newtown, of Sandy Hook Elementary, should not be lost, because if it is, maybe it is lost forever.

It was officially lost in Washington on Tuesday, lost to fear and lost to ignorance and lost to the NRA. One last time: If not a ban on assault weapons now, then when? Shame on them all.

> *"'Assault weapon' is a* purely invented term, *designed by politicians to mislead the public into thinking that consumers can buy machine guns in Wal-Mart."*

# ABC: But 'Assault Weapons' Bans Just Make Guns *Look* Different!

*Charles C.W. Cooke*

*In the following viewpoint, Charles C.W. Cooke claims that bans on so-called assault weapons are misguided because the term itself is invented. He contends that the New York Secure Ammunition and Firearms Enforcement Act, commonly known as the New York SAFE Act, which was passed into law in 2013, outlawed certain cosmetic components of guns that have nothing to do with lethality. Cooke claims that gun manufacturers will simply alter the design to get past the law. Cooke also contends that assault rifles are not even used in crimes and murders very often. Cooke is a staff writer at* National Review.

Charles C.W. Cooke, "ABC: But 'Assault Weapons' Bans Just Make Guns *Look* Different!," *National Review Online*, May 8, 2014. Copyright © 2014 National Review Online. All rights reserved. Reproduced by permission.

As you read, consider the following questions:

1. According to the author, what does "assault weapon" mean in the political world?

2. According to Cooke, the AR-15 rifle is so popular because what three groups can use it easily?

3. For what type of weapons does the FBI not bother keeping crime statistics, according to Cooke?

Headline of the day from ABC New York: "After NY Gun Control Law, Assault Rifles Only Look Different." The story:

> A month after the massacre at Sandy Hook Elementary School in 2012, New York passed a set of gun control laws that proponents touted as the toughest in the nation.
>
> Now some critics say one part of the law—the assault rifle ban—is not effective because new models being made to comply with the law are almost entirely the same as those that were banned.
>
> "The guns are exact," said Long Island gun dealer Martin Tretola.
>
> Tretola took the I-Team to the gun range to demonstrate what he says are merely cosmetic changes the SAFE Act [New York's Secure Ammunition and Firearms Enforcement Act] imposed on one of America's most popular type of rifle, the AR-15.
>
> Under the law, bayonet mounts, flash suppressors and telescoping stocks are banned, and rifles cannot have a pistol grip.
>
> But the new modified rifle is still semiautomatic. That means each squeeze of the trigger automatically loads the next round into the chamber.

For the last damn time: "Assault weapon" is a *purely invented term*, designed by politicians to mislead the public into thinking that consumers can buy machine guns in Wal-Mart. They can't. In the political world at least, "assault weapon" means nothing more or less than "semiautomatic rifle that has a few cosmetic features that we do not like." It does *not* mean "machine gun"—those have been heavily regulated since 1934, their production and importation has been banned since 1986, and one has not been used in a murder in half a century. It does *not* mean "more powerful rifle"—one can still buy much more powerful semiautomatic weapons that do not have any of the aesthetic features that the gun control brigade has decided it doesn't like. It does *not* mean "weapon that the military uses" or "especially deadly." It refers only to cosmetics.

*Of course* the rifles "only look different" now. When you ban cosmetic features, you're going to see manufacturers producing guns that look different. What did they expect?

Luckily, ABC had an academic on hand to explain the law to them:

> NYU [New York University] law professor James Jacobs, who has written extensively on gun control issues, praises portions of the SAFE Act, including expanded background checks.
>
> But he says the assault rifle ban has resulted in a remodeled gun that is no less dangerous—just less scary looking.
>
> "It differs only in how it looks, not in how it functions," Jacobs said.
>
> The law redefined an assault weapon as a semiautomatic rifle that can accept a detachable magazine and has one military-style feature such as a pistol grip or folding stock.

Note that last line. Note that the law did *not* change the "semiautomatic rifle" part, but restricted the features that one

## A Myth About Assault Weapons

Gun control supporters call "assault weapons" (and all other firearms, for that matter) "high-powered." However, a firearm's power is determined by the caliber or gauge of its ammunition; semiautomatic rifles and shotguns use the same ammunition as many other rifles and shotguns, and semiautomatic handguns use ammunition comparable to revolver ammunition. So-called "assault weapons" are much less powerful than many rifles used to hunt deer and other large game.

*National Rifle Association of America–*
*Institute for Legislative Action, "Ten Reasons*
*Why States Should Reject 'Assault Weapon' and*
*'Large' Magazine Bans," June 17, 2014.*

can add on to it—features, it apparently needs spelling out, that have absolutely nothing to do with the lethality of the weapon.

This, of course, doesn't prevent gun control types from pretending that they are doing something useful:

Yet gun control advocates say a less comfortable rifle is also a less deadly weapon.

"The legal gun looks a lot like the illegal gun," said Leah Gunn Barrett, the executive director of New Yorkers Against Gun Violence. "Does that make this law essentially cosmetic? No. These features all have specific functions."

For example, Gunn Barrett said a forward-leaning pistol grip might give a mass shooter better control over his rifle.

"The gun is still lethal," Gunn Barrett said. "Yes, it can still kill people. But it is not as easy to manipulate and fire accurately than it would be if you had a forward-leaning pistol grip."

Actually, making rifles less comfortable primarily makes it more difficult for weaker individuals to use them. This is rarely spelled out, but one of the reasons that the AR-15 is so popular is that women, the disabled, and the young can use it so easily. Far from being the weapon of choice for the American criminal, rifles of all types—not merely those designated as "assault weapons"—are almost never used in crimes, murders, or shooting sprees. As I have noted elsewhere,

> If someone is killed with a gun in America, it is almost certain that a handgun was used. Rifles of all types—not just so-called "assault rifles"—are used in around 3 percent of killings, while shotguns are used in around 3.5 percent. So rare are deaths from either rifles or shotguns that the FBI finds hands and fists causing more deaths than both combined. Handguns, on the other hand, account for almost all deaths by firearm.

Meanwhile, the use of what the government considers to be "assault" rifles is so rare in the United States that the FBI doesn't even bother to keep statistics.

Write a stupid law, you'll get a stupid outcome. Bravo, New York. Bravo.

# Periodical and Internet Sources Bibliography

*The following articles have been selected to supplement the diverse views presented in this chapter.*

| | |
|---|---|
| E.J. Dionne | "Rationalizing Gutlessness on Guns," *Washington Post*, July 25, 2012. |
| Richard A. Epstein | "Will Banning Guns Prevent Another Aurora?," *Defining Ideas*, July 24, 2012. |
| Max Fisher | "A Land Without Guns: How Japan Has Virtually Eliminated Shooting Deaths," *Atlantic*, July 23, 2012. |
| Jeffrey Goldberg | "The Case for More Guns (and More Gun Control)," *Atlantic*, November 28, 2012. |
| Katie Kieffer | "Let Women Carry Concealed Firearms on Campus," *Townhall*, January 27, 2014. |
| Judith Miller | "Treasure the Second Amendment, but Ban Assault Rifles," Newsmax, July 23, 2012. |
| Jeffrey Miron | "Strict Gun Control Will Seem Like War on Drugs," Bloomberg News, January 13, 2011. |
| Geoffrey Norman | "Gun Fights," *Weekly Standard*, July 26, 2012. |
| Eugene Volokh | "Why Bans on So-Called 'Assault Weapons' Are Unlikely to Diminish the Deaths Caused by Mass Shootings," *The Volokh Conspiracy*, December 18, 2012. |
| Kevin D. Williamson | "The Dishonest Gun-Control Debate," *National Review Online*, May 3, 2013. |

# For Further Discussion

## Chapter 1

1. The authors of the viewpoints in this chapter are talking about the same set of facts, but they come to different conclusions. Name one point of agreement shared by at least three authors, and point to a way each of their viewpoints differs from the other two authors.

2. In establishing the seriousness of the problem of gun violence, does it matter how much gun violence existed in the past? Name one author who would say no and one who would say yes. What do you think? Explain your reasoning.

## Chapter 2

1. At the heart of the debate about America's gun culture is the issue of the availability of guns. Elias Groll claims that America's gun culture leads to greater gun violence. Do you agree with Groll's argument? Explain your response.

2. Do you think Trevor Burrus would agree with Heather Mac Donald's suggestion to beef up policing in the inner cities where there are problems with gun violence? Why, or why not?

3. Abby Rapoport expresses concern that singling out mentally ill individuals as possible perpetrators of gun violence could increase stigma about mental illness, and she warns that most mentally ill people are not violent. How would Ann Coulter respond to this worry?

## Chapter 3

1. John Lott says that the number of people who obtain guns without a background check is much lower than usually charged, in part because he says that the survey

cited is from 1993, prior to the implementation of mandatory federal background checks. Based on what is discussed by Mayors Against Illegal Guns, what has changed in the ensuing years that may, in fact, mean that the number is much higher now than in 1993? Explain your answer.

2. Wayne Allyn Root claims that armed citizens prevent thousands of crimes every year by being armed. Does this commit Root to the argument that if every single citizen were armed, America would have the least violence and crime possible? Explain your reasoning.

## Chapter 4

1. Robert A. Levy argues that ending the drug war would reduce gun violence. Do you agree with Levy's argument? Why, or why not?

2. Charles C.W. Cooke calls "assault weapons" an invented term. Does this matter? Can a law simply identify certain components of guns to ban without running into the problems he claims plague New York's SAFE Act? Explain your reasoning.

# Organizations to Contact

*The editors have compiled the following list of organizations concerned with the issues debated in this book. The descriptions are derived from materials provided by the organizations. All have publications or information available for interested readers. The list was compiled on the date of publication of the present volume; the information provided here may change. Be aware that many organizations take several weeks or longer to respond to inquiries, so allow as much time as possible.*

**Brady Campaign to Prevent Gun Violence**
840 First Street, Suite 400, Washington, DC   20002
(202) 370-8101
website: www.bradycampaign.org

The Brady Campaign to Prevent Gun Violence is a nonprofit, nonpartisan organization working to make it harder for convicted felons, the dangerously mentally ill, and other such individuals to get guns. Through its network of Million Mom March chapters and other initiatives, the Brady Campaign rallies for sensible gun laws, regulations, and public policies, as well as works to educate the public about gun violence. Available at its website are numerous fact sheets, studies, and reports about gun control regulations, gun trafficking, public opinion, and other issues.

**Cato Institute**
1000 Massachusetts Avenue NW
Washington, DC   20001-5403
(202) 842-0200 • fax: (202) 842-3490
website: www.cato.org

The Cato Institute is a public policy research organization dedicated to the principles of individual liberty, limited government, free markets, and peace. The institute is dedicated to increasing and enhancing the understanding of key public policies and to realistically analyzing their impact on the afore-mentioned principles. The Cato Institute offers many publications, such as the quarterly *Regulation* magazine, the bi-monthly *Cato Policy Report*, and the periodic *Cato Journal*.

### Children's Defense Fund (CDF)

25 E Street NW, Washington, DC   20001
(800) 233-1200
e-mail: cdfinfo@childrensdefense.org
website: www.childrensdefense.org

The Children's Defense Fund (CDF) is a nonprofit child advocacy organization that works to ensure a level playing field for all American children. CDF's Protect Children, Not Guns campaign aims to protect children instead of the individual right to firearms. CDF publishes the annual "Protect Children, Not Guns" report.

### Coalition to Stop Gun Violence (CSGV)

805 Fifteenth Street, Suite 700, Washington, DC   20005
(202) 408-0061
e-mail: csgv@csgv.org
website: www.csgv.org

The Coalition to Stop Gun Violence (CSGV) is made up of forty-seven national organizations working to reduce gun violence. CSGV seeks to secure freedom from gun violence through aggressive political advocacy. CSGV has links on its website to the reports, memos, testimony, and websites of its member organizations.

### Gun Owners of America (GOA)

8001 Forbes Place, Suite 102, Springfield, VA   22151
(703) 321-8585 • fax: (703) 321-8408
website: www.gunowners.org

Gun Owners of America (GOA) is a nonprofit lobbying organization that works to preserve and defend the Second Amendment rights of gun owners. GOA helps fight court battles to protect gun owner rights and works with politicians and citizens to protect gun ranges and local gun clubs from closure by the government. GOA publishes fact sheets, including "Thirteen Reasons Why Congress Should Oppose Universal Background Checks."

## Jews for the Preservation of Firearms Ownership (JPFO)

12500 NE Tenth Place, Bellevue, WA    98005
(800) 486-6963
e-mail: jpfo@jpfo.org
website: www.jpfo.org

Jews for the Preservation of Firearms Ownership (JPFO) is a nonprofit organization with the goal of opposing and reversing gun control. JPFO works to educate the public on the danger of disarmament policies. JPFO has produced several films on the issue of gun control, including *Innocents Betrayed* and *2A Today for the USA*, and it publishes information at its website.

## National Crime Prevention Council (NCPC)

2001 Jefferson Davis Highway, Suite 901, Arlington, VA    22202
(202) 466-6272
website: www.ncpc.org

The National Crime Prevention Council (NCPC) was founded in 1982 to help keep families and their communities safe from crime. Through its programs and educational materials, the council works to teach Americans how to reduce crime and to address its causes. It provides readers with information on gun control and gun violence. The NCPC provides publications and teaching materials, as well as offers articles, brochures, and fact sheets on its website.

## National Firearms Association of Canada (NFA)

PO Box 49090, Edmonton, Alberta    T6E 6H4
   Canada
(877) 818-0393 • fax: (780) 439-4091

e-mail: info@nfa.ca
website: www.nfa.ca

The National Firearms Association of Canada (NFA) works for and with Canadian gun owners. The NFA supports legislation that reflects the needs of Canadian gun owners. The NFA publishes the *Canadian Firearms Journal*.

### National Institute of Justice (NIJ)

810 Seventh Street NW, Washington, DC   20531
(202) 307-2942
website: www.nij.gov

The National Institute of Justice (NIJ) is the research, development, and evaluation agency of the US Department of Justice, dedicated to improving knowledge and understanding of crime and justice issues through science. NIJ provides objective and independent knowledge as well as the tools to reduce crime and promote justice, particularly at the state and local levels. NIJ provides data, graphs, and reports about gun violence, available at its website.

### National Rifle Association of America (NRA)

11250 Waples Mill Road, Fairfax, VA   22030
(800) 672-3888
website: www.nra.org

The National Rifle Association of America (NRA) is America's largest organization of gun owners and a powerful pro–gun rights group. The NRA's Institute for Legislative Action lobbies against restrictive gun control legislation. In addition to fact sheets published by its Institute for Legislative Action, the NRA publishes the journals *American Rifleman, American Hunter*, and *America's 1st Freedom*.

### Second Amendment Committee

PO Box 1776, Hanford, CA   93232
(559) 584-5209 • fax: (559) 584-4084

e-mail: liberty89@libertygunrights.com
website: www.libertygunrights.com

The Second Amendment Committee, founded by a longtime gun rights activist, is a nationwide organization that aims to protect the right to keep and bear arms. The committee has authored pro-gun legislation. It has a variety of documents available at its website.

## Second Amendment Foundation (SAF)

12500 NE Tenth Place, Bellevue, WA   98005
(425) 454-7012
e-mail: info@saf.org
website: www.saf.org

The Second Amendment Foundation (SAF) is dedicated to promoting a better understanding of the constitutional heritage to privately own and possess firearms. SAF develops educational and legal action programs designed to better inform the public about the gun control debate. SAF publishes the *Journal on Firearms & Public Policy* and *Women & Guns*.

## Stop Handgun Violence (SHV)

One Bridge Street, Suite 300, Newton, MA   02458
(617) 243-8124 • fax: (617) 965-7308
website: www.stophandgunviolence.com

Stop Handgun Violence (SHV) is a nonprofit organization committed to the prevention of gun violence through public awareness and legislation, without banning guns. SHV aims to increase public awareness about gun violence through media and public education campaigns. Available at the SHV website are gun violence facts, stories, and information about SHV's media campaigns.

## Violence Policy Center (VPC)

1730 Rhode Island Avenue NW, Suite 1014
Washington, DC   20036

(202) 822-8200
website: www.vpc.org

The Violence Policy Center (VPC) is a nonprofit organization that aims to stop death and injury from firearms. VPC conducts research on gun violence in America and works to develop violence-reduction policies and proposals. VPC publishes studies on a range of gun violence issues, including "Cash and Carry: How Concealed Carry Laws Drive Gun Industry Profits."

# Bibliography of Books

| | |
|---|---|
| Ben Agger and Timothy W. Luke, eds. | *Gun Violence and Public Life.* Boulder, CO: Paradigm Publishers, 2014. |
| Glenn Beck | *Control: Exposing the Truth About Guns.* New York: Threshold Editions/Mercury Radio Arts, 2013. |
| Philip J. Cook and Kristin A. Goss | *The Gun Debate: What Everyone Needs to Know.* New York: Oxford University Press, 2014. |
| Tom Diaz | *The Last Gun: How Changes in the Gun Industry Are Killing Americans and What It Will Take to Stop It.* New York: New Press, 2013. |
| Matt Doeden | *Gun Control: Preventing Violence or Crushing Constitutional Rights?* Minneapolis, MN: Twenty-First Century Books, 2012. |
| Anthony K. Fleming | *Gun Policy in the United States and Canada: The Impact of Mass Murders and Assassinations on Gun Control.* New York: Continuum, 2012. |
| Alan Gottlieb and Dave Workman | *Shooting Blanks: Facts Don't Matter to the Gun Ban Crowd.* Bellevue, WA: Merril Press, 2011. |
| Institute of Medicine and National Research Council | *Priorities for Research to Reduce the Threat of Firearm-Related Violence.* Washington, DC: National Academies Press, 2013. |

Nicholas Johnson    *Negroes and the Gun: The Black Tradition of Arms*. Amherst, NY: Prometheus Books, 2014.

David B. Kopel    *The Truth About Gun Control*. New York: Encounter Books, 2013.

John R. Lott Jr.    *More Guns, Less Crime: Understanding Crime and Gun Control Laws*. 3rd ed. Chicago, IL: University of Chicago Press, 2010.

Scott Melzer    *Gun Crusaders: The NRA's Culture War*. New York: New York University Press, 2009.

Piers Morgan    *Shooting Straight: Guns, Gays, God, and George Clooney*. London: Ebury Press, 2013.

Grover G. Norquist    *Leave Us Alone: Getting the Government's Hands Off Our Money, Our Guns, Our Lives*. New York: Harper Collins, 2009.

Brian Anse Patrick    *Rise of the Anti-Media: In-Forming America's Concealed Weapon Carry Movement*. Lanham, MD: Lexington Books, 2010.

Gerry Souter    *American Shooter: A Personal History of Gun Culture in the United States*. Washington, DC: Potomac Books, 2012.

Robert J. Spitzer    *The Politics of Gun Control*. 6th ed. Boulder, CO: Paradigm Publishers, 2014.

France
Winddance Twine

*Girls with Guns: Firearms, Feminism, and Militarism.* New York: Routledge, 2013.

Michael Waldman

*The Second Amendment: A Biography.* New York: Simon & Schuster, 2014.

Irvin Waller

*Smarter Crime Control: A Guide to a Safer Future for Citizens, Communities, and Politicians.* Lanham, MD: Rowman & Littlefield, 2013.

Daniel W. Webster and Jon S. Vernick, eds.

*Reducing Gun Violence in America: Informing Policy with Evidence and Analysis.* Baltimore, MD: Johns Hopkins University Press, 2013.

Craig R. Whitney

*Living with Guns: A Liberal's Case for the Second Amendment.* New York: Public Affairs, 2012.

Adam Winkler

*Gunfight: The Battle Over the Right to Bear Arms in America.* New York: W.W. Norton, 2013.

# Index

## A

Abortion, 32

Access to firearms
    causes of gun violence, 63, 64, 67–70
    homicide links, 25, 67
    illegal gun trade, 73
    suicide, 25, 54
    youth violence, 38, 54, 55

Accidental shootings, 67, 99

Adults, juveniles tried as, 40

Advertising, online gun buying, 126–127

African Americans
    community aspects, 74
    concerns about gun violence, 42
    gun violence victims, rates, 14, 15, 37, 39
    young victims of gun violence, 37, 39, 73–74, 149

Age differences
    crime rate beliefs and knowledge, 29, 31
    youth gun violence and victims, 14, 15, 21, 22–24, 34–42, 67–68, 149

Alexis, Aaron, 99–100

American Civil Liberties Union (ACLU), 85

American Revolution, 69

Annie E. Casey Foundation, 78

Appalachian School of Law (Virginia), 119–120

Armed citizens
    do not reduce gun violence, 113–121
    law enforcement opinions, 110*t*, 119–120
    reduce gun violence, 107–112
    shooting of criminals, vs. police action, 109, 115

Armslist (website), 125, 126–129, 130, 131–133

Asian/Pacific Islander Americans
    concerns about gun violence, 42
    gun violence victims, rates, 39

Assassinations, 95

Assault, rates, 27, 37

Assault weapons
    bans and ban proposals, 66, 88, 120, 139–140, 152–153, 154, 156–158, 167, 168–171, 170*t*
    bans are misguided, 172–176
    construction, 173–176
    NRA statements, 175
    usage, 120, 152–153, 157, 161, 167, 168–169

Australia, 58, 163

Availability of guns. *See* Access to firearms; Gun laws; Illegal gun trade

## B

Background checks
    history and legislation, 25, 95–96, 132, 133, 136, 141–143, 147, 158–160

online gun buying investigations, 127–131

# D

Daniel, Zina, 130

Databases
gun owners, 136
mentally ill, 87, 88, 89–90, 98, 121
*See also* National Instant Criminal Background Check System (NICS)

Davidson Middle School (Southgate, Michigan), 54

Democratic leadership
Chicago, Illinois, and gun control, 46, 47–49
gun control wariness, 121
national gun control support, 66

Demographic changes, and crime rates, 27, 31–32, 33

Dinkins, David, 139–140

Disease deaths, 37, 38, 67

*District of Columbia v. Heller* (2008), 69–70, 136, 146, 155, 158

Domestic violence
gun violence locations and rates, 15
homicides, 58, 101, 130, 149
private gun sales to abusers, 129–130
protective order records, 25
*See also* Family problems, and youth gun violence

Drinking and guns, 116, *118*

Drug Enforcement Administration (DEA), 160

Drug legalization, 160

Drug trade
related violence, 69, 71–75, 160
shifts/changes, 24, 31

Drug use
causes of gun violence, 63
correlation with gun violence, 89, 90, 97, 101

# E

Early release, prison, 64

Eastern Florida State College (Palm Bay, Florida), 52

Economic costs, incarceration, 40, 41, 74

Economic cycles and suicide, 25

Education. *See* Education standards; Educational programs, anti-violence; Public schools, critiques

Education standards, 48, 71, 74

Educational Fund to Stop Gun Violence, 101–102

Educational programs, anti-violence, 25, 59

El Salvador, 18

Emanuel, Rahm, 47, 108

England, 18

Europe
demographic shifts, 33
gun registration and bans, 139

Everytown for Gun Safety, 50, 122

Extremism, 63–64

# F

Family problems, and youth gun violence, 76, 77, 79, 80

Popular culture influence, 63, 64
Population rates
    birth rate shifts, 32
    changes, and crime rate de-
        clines, 27, 31–32, 33
    death rate (overall), 36
    global, 67
    millennial generation, 42
Possessions offenses
    Fix Gun Checks Act (bill),
        141–142
    proactive policing, and posi-
        tive effects, 76, 80, 166
    youth crimes, 39–40
Poverty rates, 48
Poynter, Joseph, 54
Prediction of violence, 59–60, 79,
    89
Prevention efforts, gun violence
    complicated nature, 56, 57–58
    education, 25, 59
    mental health angles, 60
    methods, 24–25, 31, 59–60
    proactive policing, 76, 79–80,
        162, 164–166
    public support, 29
    scientifically proven methods,
        59
    via armed citizens, 107, 108–
        109
    youth focus, 21, 25, 59
    See also Background checks;
        Gun control debate; Gun
        laws; Law enforcement
Prison. See Incarceration
Privacy issues
    mentally ill, 82, 98, 101
    personal gun transfer rights,
        135, 136, 142–143

Private gun sales and giving
    background checks or lack
        thereof, 99, 104, 105, 124–
        134, 135, 158–160
    existing laws, 137–138
    gun shows, 73, 140–141
    investigations, 125–134
    loophole needs to be closed,
        122–134
    rights protection, 135–143
    transfers, background checks,
        125
    transfers, taxation, 95
    See also Black market weapons
Proactive policing policies, 76,
    79–80, 162, 164–166
Product recalls, 129
Prohibition, 73, 95
Project Safe Neighborhoods
    (Chicago, Illinois), 165–166
"Promise Zones," 77–78
Property crimes, 32–33
Psychotic episodes, 83–84
Public health aspect of gun vio-
    lence
    approach to violence preven-
        tion, 25, 59
    gun violence is public health
        concern, 20–25, 35, 37–38,
        113, 120–121
Public health programs, 25, 59
Public opinion
    background checks for gun
        purchases, 42
    causes of gun violence, 63–64,
        108
    felons, 109–110
    gun control, 96, 108, 170t, 171
    gun culture and public safety,
        41–42
    gun ownership, 41